INDIAN HEROES

INDIAN HEROES

J. WALKER McSPADDEN

THOMAS Y. CROWELL COMPANY
New York

To the

BOY SCOUTS OF MONTCLAIR
BEGINNING WITH "UNCLE"

This Volume of the Original Scouts of America
Is Dedicated

PREFACE

WHAT were the Indians like in the days when our land was being explored and settled by the Europeans? Endless stories and pictures have tried to tell the tale, but always from the side of the white man. The Indian was a savage who fought savagely, we have been told, and the white man was always right.

Not long ago an article was written by an Indian princess. She complained that, while stories and books sometimes present her people's side of history fairly, television and motion pictures continue to perpetuate the stereotypes of the Indian. He was bloodthirsty and vengeful, and the phrase, "the only good Indian is a dead Indian," is still being quoted. Many of us, however, not only have delved into our histories a bit, but have met the Indians of today both East and West, and have learned to admire the way they live in the remnants of land still left them by our covetous selves.

I paid a visit to the Cherokee fair a few years ago at the Cherokee reservation in the Great Smoky Mountains of North Carolina. For centuries before the white men came this tribe hunted game, raised some crops, and had arts and crafts and laws of their own. They resisted the invaders in their mountain fastnesses so successfully that a portion of the tribe was permitted to remain. One of them, Sequoya, later invented the first alphabet used by his tribe, and his name also was given to the giant trees of California—the sequoias.

It was a fine autumn day when my party came to their fair. The settlement looked much like any other one—scattered homes dotting the hillside, tidy farmlands, well-kept livestock, a "contented" look. At the fair itself we saw the usual jellies, cakes, pickles, and also samples of truly Indian work such as rugs and shawls. We saw the Corn Dance being led by an agile man of eighty-five. When I commented on his skill, I was informed that "he ought to be good; he's been dancing that since he was five years old!"

A visit to the Blackfoot tribe near Glacier National Park shows another happy, prosperous farming people. In the Southwest, the Navajos, once a fierce lot of warriors, are tending their sheep on land so arid that it is a marvel they can make a living, for both the grazing space and the water rights are parceled out by the government with none too generous hand. These pictures can be added to by every traveler who crosses our continent today. The Indian is friendly, quiet, uncomplaining—yet how few of us still understand him!

Of course the Indian of a century or so ago was a different sort of fellow when he got into his war paint. He was fighting to keep his homelands. Who wouldn't do as much? He had met these queer strangers in friendly fashion when they stepped from their huge winged canoes, but all too soon he learned that the newcomers were not friends; instead they came to take the land and enslave the people. It was said of the Pilgrim Fathers that they first "fell upon their knees and then upon the aborigines." As the English settlements pushed westward in what is now Massachusetts, the Indians, who had tried to be friends, were driven farther and farther back. The same was true in Virginia and all along the coast; later in the opening of the West. It is all in our history books, but written by the white man, who has not had much to say about broken treaties—broken on our side—and other bits of sharp dealing which we would label "treachery" if we were on the other side of the fence.

We read of how Osceola, the Seminole chieftain, was seized in Florida under a flag of truce. Geronimo, the last of the fighting Apaches, surrendered under promise that his people would be well treated, but instead they were sent as pris-

PREFACE

oners to Alabama and put to hard labor. Again when Sitting Bull, one of the last of the fighting Sioux, fled to Canada after the wiping out of Custer's men at the Little Big Horn, he replied to United States agents who came to conclude a treaty with him: "I cannot trust you. You speak with two tongues."

I cite merely a few instances to show that there can be another side to any story. The object of this book is to present true tales of adventure from the Indians' point of view. Let them speak for themselves. Insofar as they paint either party as the aggressor or the wrongdoer, they are merely documents torn from the pages of history. I have fictionized minor incidents or dialogue, but have otherwise set down serious records.

And the stories are not all somber. It is pleasant to find evidences of good faith and fair dealing on both sides. You might say that in the first story, telling of the sale of Manhattan Island, the price agreed upon—about twenty-four dollars in present money—was cheap; but the Indians thought it a fine trade! And the tale of Penn's treaty with his native friends down under a big oak near Philadelphia—a treaty which was faithfully kept for over half a century —is another example of honorable dealing. The stories of how Pocahontas befriended the Vir-

PREFACE

ginians, and of Squanto and the Pilgrims are parts of our American tradition.

When we use the term *American,* let us by all means include the men and women and girls and boys who lived here and loved their homeland long before we intruders came. Let us not begrudge them their rightful place in our history, nor begrudge them the scattered parcels of land styled "reservations" where they can eat the bread of peace and dream of the vanished days of freedom.

J. W. McS.

CONTENTS

CHAPTER ONE

THE MANHATTANS AND THEIR ISLAND

"IT is a strange thing that has been seen. A great flying canoe that moves along the water without paddles or the efforts of men. It has white wings that stretch up into the sky and catch the winds of morning. I myself would not have believed, had I not seen the monster with these two eyes!"

The speaker was an Indian runner, footsore and weary, who had scarce taken time to catch breath before giving the astounding tidings. The circle of braves who listened shook their heads in doubt. Behind them clustered the squaws and children, who set up a chattering among themselves that went unrebuked, while the men by questions to the runner sought to learn what it was all about. But he had exhausted his small stock of news with the first breath.

Wamba,[1] the lad of ten summers, son of the old chief, Mahatone, listened to the fragments of talk eagerly. Their village, Nappeckamack,

[1] The name, "Wamba," is fictitious.

1

lay at the foot of a chain of hills facing a lordly
river. Across the stream lay still higher hills
which rose range upon range until they became
mountains. For which reason Wamba's people
called themselves Manhattans—the people of
the island of hills. To the south of them lay
their island, a tongue-shaped point of land
washed on the east and west by wide streams
leading to the "great water" beyond.

Such was Manhattan Island of over three centuries ago, when Wamba was a boy. And it was
at the southern tip of this island that Nando, the
runner, said that he had seen the strange flying
canoe.

After much excited powwow Mahatone, the
chief, lifted his hand and at once the babel ceased.

"These are strange words that Nando brings
to our ears," he said; "and Nando knows the
fate of liars. Their tongues are fed to the eagles.
As for me, I would go to see this marvel for
myself."

"And I." "And I," came from a dozen throats,
as the men in the circle extended their hands
toward the sky.

Without further parley the braves made ready
for their journey. It was but the work of a few
moments. Each took a small bag of parched
corn for food, and his weapons—bows and arrows chiefly, with here and there a spear or a

tomahawk. They marched light, their bodies naked save for a breech-cloth glistening in the sun.

As their leader emerged from his wigwam, he looked into the eager, upturned face of Wamba.

"Take me with you, father," he pleaded. "I, too, would see the giant canoe with wings."

"It is a day's march," answered Mahatone, "and the trail is rough. We cannot be hindered."

"My father wants me to grow up to become a great chief," said Wamba. "Let me prove to him that my legs are as tough as the young deer's."

The old chief looked proudly at his son. "Come!" he said.

Flushed with delight Wamba seized his small bow and arrows, and fell in line at the end of the single file of warriors—the envy of every other·lad in the village.

After following a trail leading close beside the wide river for a few miles they emerged upon another and narrower stream flowing into it and blocking their path to the south. Here, however, canoes lay hidden in readiness and it was the work of but a few moments to launch them and paddle to the other side. Again were the canoes carefully hidden, lest they fall into the hands of their enemies, the fierce Mohawks, and the march was resumed.

It led them the length of Manhattan Island where in the years to come the great city of New York was to rise. But on this September day in the year 1609—reckoning by the paleface calendar—the land through which the band of Indians threaded their way was a tangled wilderness, a royal hunting ground such as the Indians loved. At its upper end where they began their march rose a series of steep hills and deep valleys lying parallel to the river which flowed out toward the sea. The ground lifted steeply from the river at first, but gradually sloped toward sea level, and about halfway down the length of the island deep inlets, marshes and bayous began to appear. These made marching more difficult and necessitated wide detours. But Mahatone and his warriors did not hesitate, as trails led in several directions. Their tribe had hunted this land for many generations.

At times they would let themselves carefully down small cliffs where a single misstep would give them a nasty fall. Again they would force their way through thickets of blackberry, raspberry, and other prickly bushes. Once they stopped before a particularly inviting wild grapevine which clambered to the top of a tree.

The berries, just ripe, hung in heavy clusters, and they ate their fill.

Back in the thickets they knew that many a wild animal lurked—wolves, foxes, martens, bears,—while down toward the marshes the beavers had their home. But to-day the Indians did not turn aside to hunt. After the briefest of rests they pressed on, as they wished to reach the tip of the island before sunset. As they resumed their march Mahatone looked sharply at Wamba. The boy drew himself up alertly and looked back, seemingly as fresh as when they had begun their march. The chief grunted a single word of encouragement as he took up the trail anew.

Toward the middle of the afternoon they found their path once more blocked by water. An arm of the sea, at high tide, stretched right across the island from west to east. Many years later when the white man had filled in and dredged this channel, it was called Canal Street. This time the men on the trail did not bother with canoes. They were hot and tired, so one after another they plunged into the water and swam to the other side, Wamba with them. They climbed out dripping and shook themselves, much as dogs do, and found the salt water refreshing.

A short distance below they came upon some

rude clearings, where grew maize, pumpkins, beans, and a few other vegetables, tended by squaws who lived in the village near the tip of the island. This village resembled their own, Nappeckamack. In summer there were many tepees and other rough outdoor shelters. But in winter they lived in comfort in long cabins sheathed with bark. These houses were arched over by young saplings and thus had rounded or cone-shaped roofs. They were quite long, the principal one being over a hundred feet, and housing several families. In cold weather a large fire was built on a stone hearth in the center, and a hole in the roof allowed the smoke to escape.

As they neared this village they saw signs everywhere of the greatest confusion. Men, women, and children were running back and forth, dogs were barking, and the arrival of Mahatone passed almost unnoticed. All were talking about the strange ship which lay at anchor at the tip of the island, and its stranger sailors. Mahatone and the head chief exchanged salutes and withdrew apart to discuss the unheard-of situation.

"Some of our men have already visited this winged canoe, and been peacefully received. The palefaces who are on board have told us by signs —as they speak a queer and barbarous tongue that nobody understands—that we may come again at the next sunrise. They are not of the same hue as ourselves, but pale, like sick men.

"Who they are, or whether they come as friends or foes, we do not know; but it behooves us to show the smiling face until we learn more about them. Some of our old men say they are akin to the gods, and that the thunders and lightnings of heaven are concealed within their vessel. They say this coming has been foretold for many moons."

"So naught can be done this night?" asked Mahatone.

"My brother has travelled far and needs food and sleep. At the rising of the sun we will go together to see this wonder."

And thus it was decided. The next morning found many Indians down at the point of land looking south toward the bay. There indeed lay the strange and fearsome ship. It rested lightly on the waves, riding high out of the water and seeming higher because of a lofty and square stern. This bore the device of a half moon, and they learned afterwards it betokened the name of the vessel, the *Half Moon*. A flag surmounted the stern, with three stripes, one orange, one white, and one blue. Tall trees (masts) stood in the center of the boat, and from their square limbs hung what seemed to be wings, only they were now furled as the ship tugged at its anchor.

With the coming of Mahatone and the other chiefs to the water's edge, preparations were at once made to visit the stranger. Half a dozen canoes went first, the leading one carrying Mahatone and Wamba. Queer, white-faced men, —as the other chief had said—and whose bodies were completely concealed by loose-fitting garments, stood at the ship's rail watching their approach. Some of them carried iron weapons with long, shiny barrels across their shoulders. Others had knives, and one commanding looking man wore a long sword. However, the visitors made no hostile move; in fact, beckoned them to approach, and even threw down ropes over the ship's side, to aid them to come on board. But after the first six canoes had come, they waved the others away.

Wamba heard afterwards that the palefaces were wary because of a surprise attack made upon them the day before. On their way up from the lower bay to the upper bay, while a smaller boat had taken a party of them ashore to explore the land, some hostile Indians had sent a shower of arrows at them, and killed one, an arrow piercing his throat. His name was Coleman, and as he was the first white man to lose his life in these waters, the others never forgot him but called the point of land where he was buried "Coleman's Point," and thus it was called ever after.

Wamba stepped aboard this great canoe and looked about him in wide-eyed wonder. Even his father and the older men made no attempt to conceal their astonishment. They trod upon a square deck cluttered by many things which were as new to them as if they had come from the abode of the Great Spirit himself. The men themselves so queerly dressed and with beards on their faces were indeed beings from another world. The Indians never wore beards, but carefully plucked out any hairs which marred their faces.

Wamba saw his father go up to the big man who wore the sword and had a sort of kettle upon his head, and make signs of peace and greeting to him. These were returned, and as best they could they tried to converse with each other by signs. The white leader was trying to find out which of the two arms of the sea to follow, and Mahatone pointed to the one at the left of the island, as they faced north. "How far did it go?" the white man seemed to say. Mahatone made several wide sweeps with his arms, tracing the course of the sun from east to west. It was a journey of several days, maybe a moon.

By and by as they talked in silence, the paleface caught sight of Wamba, and beckoned him to approach. He came shyly forward, not knowing what to expect. The man smiled at him and reached into a pocket in his full trousers, bringing to view a small hunting knife which—wonder on wonders!—folded away cunningly within a handle so that the blade was always hidden and protected. The man extended it to him. "For you," his eyes said. Wamba took it and nearly cut himself in his eagerness to open and shut the blade as he had seen the stranger do. Then he fairly capered around the deck in his delight. Wouldn't the other lads envy him—and even the braves! He was a person of distinction from that day forth! And he was forever the friend of this big man, whom later they learned to call Hudson—Henry Hudson.

Then Mahatone and his men in turn received little gifts—beads, chains, ornaments of brass and tin, which they lost no time in donning proudly. One was given a tin cup and this he tied by a thong around his neck and wore as a badge of distinction upon his breast. The men were then told by signs to depart and make room for others, which they did reluctantly, as their eyes had not yet taken in all the wonders and they did not know what lay below decks.

Other Indians and their families came and went all that autumn day. Some of the squaws brought great baskets full of dried corn and beans, and were rewarded with bright bits of cloth—perhaps a piece of calico with gaudy figures upon it and large enough to make a scanty skirt or apron—a treasure of tremendous value in their eyes. Some of the men brought fresh fish. At sunset on that day, Hudson and his men were weary from much waving of arms and smiling; but they had a goodly store of fresh food and, better still, they had apparently made friends with the people of Manhattan Island.

The *Half Moon* lay at anchor here for several days, and some of the men from it went ashore to pay a return visit to their Indian friends. They were received with much state in the large council house. Soon, spoken words began to be exchanged between them, and this enabled Henry Hudson to learn a little more about the land. He decided to follow the great river leading toward the north, and he finally persuaded Mahatone to come with him for a few days and bring Wamba. As soon as the boy learned of this plan, he was delighted. He looked upon this white captain as almost a god, and Hudson, on his part, took a great fancy to the lad, who followed him about with worshipful eyes.

One day before they set sail, Wamba saw the greatest marvel of all. Mahatone had asked about the odd-looking weapons which the men carried. They had long, round barrels which were hollow, and unless they were useful as war-clubs, he could not make out their purpose. Hudson smiled, and as they followed the trail toward the water he pointed to a squirrel on the branch of an oak tree. Then he gave a command to one of his men, who was a noted marksman. The man raised the weapon, pointed it toward the little animal, and the next moment a terrific noise with smoke and fire caused the Indians to fall back in every direction and almost drop to the ground. The squirrel was hurled from the tree and lay dead at their feet.

As soon as Mahatone could summon his speech, he muttered: "Strange medicine! Strange and powerful medicine!"

From that day Wamba had no more doubts. He *knew* that Captain Hudson was a god!

For nine days the *Half Moon* sailed up the river, which later was called by Hudson's own name. At night they cast anchor, perhaps under the shadow of some towering mountain. At other times the river would widen out into a good-sized lake, enshrouded with mists, like a curtain of mystery shrouding the unknown. Wamba had the run of the ship and found constantly new things to engage his interest. He was shown little rooms below deck in which the men slept or kept their stores. He saw huge iron things peeping out of portholes, and was told that they could make thunder a hundred times as loud as the guns carried by the men.

Every day Indians paddled out to the ship to trade. They offered fine furs as well as fresh meat, vegetables, and fruits. Like Wamba, many of them looked upon the white men as gods.

On the ninth day, Hudson found the channel becoming narrow and so shallow that his ship ran the risk of going aground. So he cast anchor and rested before turning back. He had been trying to find a northwest passage across to the Pacific, and saw that he was barred. Then Mahatone came to him and said:

"The Indians who dwell on these shores wish to welcome the great white chief, and have made a feast in his honor. Will he come?"

Hudson looked searchingly into the eyes of the other, and just then Wamba slipped up and rested his hand confidingly within the big fist of the captain. He glanced down at his little friend and said: "I will come."

And so down from the deck of the *Half Moon* went the captain and certain of his men, with Wamba and his father. The ground rose steeply from the water, although the highest of the mountains had been passed by. They were near the site of the later city of Albany, but on this day of Hudson's visit only a little Indian village broke the stillness of the primeval forest. He himself later told of this feast, just as it must have looked to Wamba's eyes. This is what he wrote about it:

I went ashore in one of their canoes with an old man who was chief of forty men and women, whom I found in a house made of the bark of trees, and was exceeding smooth and well finished within, and all round about. I found there a great quantity of Indian corn and beans, and indeed there lay to dry, near the house, of those articles, as much as would load three ships, beside what was still growing in the fields. When we went to the house two mats were spread to sit on, and immediately eatables were brought to us in wooden bowls well made, and two men were sent off with their bows and arrows to kill wild fowl, who soon returned with two pigeons. They also killed immediately a fat dog, and in a little time skinned it with shells they got out of the water.

Whether or not Captain Hudson liked his dish of "fat dog," he did not say. His ship lay at anchor there for several days, while a boat was sent farther up to try out the channel. They came back and reported that the channel rapidly grew shallower and narrower, so he reluctantly made plans to run back. Before he hoisted sail, he gave a return dinner on board to his hosts, and delighted them with beads and other trinkets. But the thing that caused Wamba the most astonishment was something that happened to the old chief. As the food was passed around, Wamba observed one of the sailors take a flagon and pour from it a fiery looking liquid. Hudson drank some of it, and made signs to the rest to do likewise. The Indians tasted it very gingerly and coughed and sputtered—all save the old chief who lifted his cup high, as he had seen the captain do, and drank a deep potion. Very soon he began to look wildly about him and jabber excitedly. Then his head fell over on his arms and he lost consciousness. The others grew panicky at this further exhibition of the white man's magic. They laid the old man down on the deck and sought to revive him, but without success. Some looked angrily at Hudson and they might have attacked him, had not Wamba, running up to him, asked by signs, "Is he dead?"

Captain Hudson smiled at them all reassuringly. "Leave him until tomorrow's sun," he said, "and the Great Spirit will restore him."

They went ashore with laggard steps and sullen looks. Hudson's men kept strict guard that night against surprise, and when the sun rose next day, sure enough the old chief sat up and looked around him dazedly. Some food restored his drooping spirits, and he went back to the village a great hero.

Because of this marvel the Indians called the

liquor "fire-water," and later came to like its effects and demand it from the traders. Hudson had unwittingly set a bad example.

Wamba and his father remained with the ship on its journey downstream, proving very useful as interpreters. The voyage back to Manhattan Island was made without special incident until they neared Nappeckamack, Wamba's home. As they sailed along, on a beautiful October afternoon, two or three canoes filled with warriors made for the ship and signalled that they wished to come aboard.

"Careful, Captain! Mohawks!" said Wamba in a low voice; and his father coming hastily up corroborated this.

Hudson stepped to the rail and motioned them back. A shower of arrows greeted him, one or two coming within inches of his head. He sought shelter and ordered his men to fire. Then indeed was Wamba terrified to see the flash of the muskets and hear their roar. Two or three men in the canoes fell and lay still. The others, after hesitating, came on again. Suddenly through a porthole the black nose of a big gun was thrust, and to Wamba it seemed as if the whole heavens had fallen. He clutched wildly at the rail for support, and as soon as the smoke had cleared away, he saw that one canoe had disappeared. A great hole had been made in it so that it foundered. The water was filled with scrambling figures, while the other canoes made haste to return to the sheltering banks.

The terrible Mohawks, the dread of all the other tribes, had met their match at last.

If Wamba started on this wonderful voyage thinking that his captain was more than mortal, he stepped ashore firmly convinced of it. With the return to the Manhattans came the final leave-taking, as the *Half Moon* made ready to go out again on the great waters. Wamba's regret at this farewell would have been tenfold, had he realized that he would never see his beloved captain again.

Back at the village he found himself a person of distinction, although but a lad. Everyone wished to see his knife, and listen to his tales about the palefaces. It was hard for them to believe many of the strange happenings, but when his father would nod his head in proof they could only wonder.

About this time, runners from the north came down with other wild stories. They said that another party of palefaces had entered the long, narrow lake from the north and had done battle with the Iroquois, the allies of the Mohawks, and slain many of them with their thunder-sticks. This was the story which came to the Indians of Champlain's excursion down the lake

which now bears his name. The same year
(1609) which witnessed Hudson's arrival was
also the time of his memorable visit. It is not
strange that the scouts and runners had many
unbelievable stories to tell around the council
fires. Surely the Great Spirit must have something in store for them, to bring both visits from
the palefaces within the same year.

Although Wamba's captain never came back,
other ships, which the Indians came to know as
Dutch, came one after another, beginning the
very next summer. Their crews were friendly
with the Manhattans, and seemed most interested
in securing the pelts of animals. The Indians
parted with these for a few trinkets very willingly. They esteemed the furs only for their
warmth, and could get more at any time by going
on a hunt. The forests teemed with game. The
Dutch, on their part, went back home with cargoes of much desired and valuable skins. Presently a thriving business had sprung up, and the
sight of a ship in the bay was a common thing
to Wamba's people.

As he grew to manhood, a trading post on the
tip of the island grew also and became a town.
But Wamba saw that it was not like the villages
of his people. This one was made of burnt clay
called bricks, or perhaps stone, or perhaps large
logs. The houses reached floor upon floor and

had big roofs. One was made into a fort, but a much stronger fort than any of the Indians', and big guns were mounted in it. Wide roadways were laid out, such as his people had never seen before, and, stranger still, they were paved with brick or stone. But he soon saw the wisdom of this, for even in wet weather their wheeled wagons could go along safely. The first of these wagons, however, nearly caused a riot, as a wheel was something entirely new to the Indians. They themselves dragged their goods along the ground on poles.

When Wamba's father, Mahatone, passed over to the Happy Hunting Grounds, Wamba, now a man grown, was made chief. One tribe after another gave him fealty, until all the Manhattans acknowledged him. He had learned to speak Dutch fluently and came and went freely in New Amsterdam, as their town was called.

One day the Governor of the colony, Peter Minuit by name, invited Wamba to dinner and then broached a subject that lay in his mind.

"We are friends, Wamba," he said; "let us always remain so."

"My brother's speech is pleasant," replied Wamba. "Ever since the coming of my captain, I have wished to be friends with the white man."

"Good," said Governor Minuit. "But where two people hold the same ground, there is bound to be jealousy and strife. We wish to live on peaceful terms with you, but as our town becomes larger, it will take up more and more of your ground. This is not right, unless you let us have the land. Why not sell it to us?"

Wamba paused. "How much land do you want?" he asked.

The Governor looked down at his pipe, to veil the crafty look in his eye.

"Would you sell us the whole of Manhattan Island?" he asked.

Wamba was taken aback and showed it. "Our island—all of it?" he ejaculated. "It has been the hunting ground of my people for many generations."

"You have also many long reaches of hunting land to the north," replied Minuit. "You can journey for many days before you reach their limits. This island of Manhattan is narrow. It is hilly in spots and swampy in others. It is not of much value and perhaps never will be. But we will give you a chest of treasure for it. What say you?"

Wamba considered. "I must talk with my people," he said at length. "I will tell you what they say."

In a council of his head men, Wamba laid the proposition before them, but without urging. He weighed its advantages and its disadvantages.

"We will part with a choice hunting ground," he said, "but we will gain treasure, and we will also make of the Dutch our allies to protect us from the Mohawks."

After much powwow and many pipes of tobacco they decided to sell the land, and Wamba reported this to the Governor. The latter was delighted and lost no time in concluding the trade. He sent surveyors around the borders of the island, and its area was roughly computed. Then on a certain day a company of Indians and another company of Dutch met on a point of land overlooking the Hudson. Minuit and Wamba stood side by side. At their feet lay a large ship's chest, and when one of the traders opened it the Indians could hardly conceal their delight, for it was filled to the brim with beads, buttons, chains, mirrors, buckles, and other objects which glittered and sparkled in the sun.

The Governor stooped over and carelessly ran his fingers through the treasure. He let it trickle through his fingers and fall in tinkling cascades.

"All this will I give you in exchange for the island," he said with a sweep of his arm which went from east to west.

Wamba looked at the other chiefs and they nodded assent. They could scarcely wait to adorn themselves with this finery.

"It is well," said Wamba. "Take the land. It is yours."

And thus was consummated one of the most important trades in history. Manhattan Island, now built from one end to the other with fine buildings worth untold millions, was obtained from its first owners for trinkets valued at about sixty guilders—or some twenty-four dollars in the money of to-day. But with the later value of their land Wamba and his people were not concerned.

"The white man needs this land worse than we do," they said. "He has offered us rich treasure for it, and he has sworn friendship with us. It is well!"

CHAPTER TWO

STRANGE tidings had come to the tribesmen of Powhatan. It was reported by the swift runners that a great canoe, larger than their council house, had come to their shores. It had no paddles, but was borne along by the winds of heaven. Some men pale of face and clad in curious armor had come ashore in small boats to spy out the land. All day they had wandered about—so the scouts said—disturbing the game and asking no leave to come thus on the Indian's land.

Powhatan, the great chief, had listened gravely to these reports. Now he interrupted to ask a question. "Did these strangers meet with any of our people?" he asked.

"No," admitted one of the runners. "Although we watched their every move, they saw not so much as a shadow of our little finger. But these pale-faced men!—they are like children in the woods. They crash through noisily, leaving a broad trail that a buffalo could follow. They are not keen of vision or scent. Our braves had not the slightest trouble in keeping out of their sight."

"Did they go back to their large canoe?" asked the sachem.

"Yes, but not until a wonderful thing happened. Our braves had crept up in the grass behind them—as many as all the fingers on my two hands, and as many more. Like serpents we crept, and the palefaces did not even know that we were near. Our bows and arrows were carried in our mouths. Just before the interlopers reached the shore we rose up and let fly at them with our arrows. One man fell, proving that they are but mortal, as we are, but the others quickly turned and pointed long, straight sticks at us. Then flashes of fire burst forth from each of these sticks, and a loud crash like thunder. We knew then that their gods must be angry with us, so hastened away to report this strange thing to you."

Powhatan listened gravely. He was a stern, majestic looking chief some sixty years old. By his prowess he had won the leadership of all the tribes in this country, which was later to be called Virginia. At least thirty tribes yielded to his sway and called him king. These coast tribes were superior to others. They were tall, well formed, and of lighter hue. Their villages were well constructed, with houses of bark, the council house being quite large. Powhatan's court was in the largest town of all, near the falls of a river which the white men were later to call the "James." Now the land and streams bore only Indian names, and the natives who dwelt round about were naturally upset and suspicious at this unexpected visit of outsiders.

"I have heard only once before of such a happening," said Powhatan, speaking slowly—but every brave and squaw froze to attention when he began to speak; even the dogs remaining silent. "When I was a young brave, on the coastland to the south of us one and then two large canoes with white wings were seen. They came up within the sheltering waters and soon began to build a town there—though it was not like our towns, but stupidly built of logs, so that they could not take it away with them again. After the great canoe sailed away, evil days fell upon those left behind. Their town was blotted out and they were taken captive into the wilderness. There was one white papoose among them. Since that day, now many moons ago, our land has been left undisturbed. These mischief-makers must be from the same country overseas."

A younger brother of the chief then signified that he would speak. It was Opecancanough, a fierce and daring fighter, who already secretly aspired to the head chiefship.

"I will take a picked company of my braves," he said, "and dog the footsteps of these pale-faces, if again they come ashore. Nor will we run away from their thundersticks."

"So be it," commanded Powhatan, with a wave of his hand, to end the council.

On his way out a little hand was shyly thrust into his and he turned to look into the eager face of his favorite child, a girl of ten. Her dark eyes, usually laughing, now had the look of sober inquiry.

"What is it, Sportive One?" asked her father, his usually gruff voice taking on a gentler tone.

"I would know more about the palefaces—and the little lost papoose," she begged.

"I do not know of a surety, and the tale is not for your small ears," evaded her father.

The child looked disappointed but from the tone of her father's voice she did not dare press her inquiry. Years later when she had learned more about the white men, she heard the tale to which he had alluded—the lost colony of Roanoke. Howbeit, the fate of the "papoose," Virginia Dare, the first white child born in America, was never known.

Powhatan's own little girl was called "Pocahontas," which in their tongue meant the "Sportive One," for she was fond of sports and games of all kinds and was hardly still a minute. She could run, jump, turn handsprings, climb, and swim as well as any of the boys—better than most of them. She had been christened Matoaka, but soon came to be called only Pocahontas.

During the next few days she thought and dreamed of nothing else but these wonderful white strangers. Indeed, the whole village buzzed about them. Curiosity and excitement were kept at fever heat by the reports of scouts who daily came to Powhatan. The white visitors had been undeterred by the first attack made upon them, he was told. The very next day a small boat had come still farther up their river, but the strangers were more wary and kept a sharp lookout, their weapons in their hands. A party of Indians enjoying an oyster roast on the shore had taken to their heels on their approach, and the white men had sat calmly down and enjoyed the feast.

The next report was still more disquieting. Two days' march upstream, if one went afoot, the white men had come ashore in force, on a jutting point of land, and it was evident that they were preparing to build one of their towns.

"Why they are building there," said the scout scornfully, "is more than we can fathom. The ground is low and marshy, and there is no good drinking water. There will be much sickness, if the palefaces build there."

This scout's opinion proved only too true in the years to come. The place of settlement, called Jamestown, was convenient to the boats but low and unhealthful. An Indian would never have chosen it for a dwelling-place.

Other messengers came in day by day telling of the progress made, so that Powhatan knew as much about the aspect of the new town as if he had seen it with his own eyes. The new-comers were busily at work cutting down trees, clearing the ground, and putting up log cabins. Next they constructed a palisade or high fence of young tree trunks and limbs, and as the point was almost an island, the only land approach from one side was well protected. In that respect, at any rate, the Indians had to admit that the white men had chosen well.

Then came further disturbing news. A party of white men was coming by boat far up the river. For six days they sailed or rowed until the shallow waters stopped them. Here they came ashore and performed a queer ceremony. They affixed a brass plate to a large tree, and then fired off a salute with their guns. After they had gone, the watching Indians crept up cautiously and looked at the strange plate. They could not make it out, and being "bad medicine," they left it alone. The plate read—for others who could read Latin—"Jacobus Rex." It was a formal claim to all the country round about, on behalf of the English king, James. If Powhatan had understood its meaning, he would not have delayed in making war. As it was, while he resented the white man's coming upon his land, he contented himself with watching and waiting the opportune time to strike.

Indeed, at the very time that this excursion was being made up the James River, a surprise attack was made on the new settlement. One boy was killed and seventeen men wounded. The natives were driven off, but the settlers realized that they must lose no time in completing their fort and palisades.

As for the Indians, when Opecancanough returned from the warpath, a council was held with Powhatan and the chiefs in his confederacy. After much powwow they decided to play a waiting game.

"It is now summer-time and food is plentiful," they said; "but soon the wild fowl will fly to the south, and there will be no more corn. Our scouts say that the white men's crops are poor and that they are laying up little for the winter. Let us wait until cold and hunger pinch them."

And so they did. The white men completed their fortifications and felt secure. There were many idlers among them and they began to take life easy. Would not another shipload of supplies reach them at any time?—they reasoned. Instead of laying up supplies, they lived well and gave no thought to the winter. A huge kettle was kept hanging over a central fire, giving off many a savory odor of wild turkey or other game. One might help himself at any time. But one autumn morning they awoke to find frost on the ground. The wild fowl no longer came down the river. There was four-footed game back in the forest, but there were also lurking natives. The big kettle soon ceased to give off its pleasant smells, and was reduced to cooking a daily stint of barley; for the promised ship had not come.

All these things the waiting Indians knew quite as well as the distressed settlers. "Ahyah!" they said, wagging their heads, "We told you so!" But when the reports came back to the council house, there was one small auditor who did not smile. Pocahontas listened and could find in her heart only pity for the strangers.

In particular, she began to hear of one—a brave warrior who had a bushy beard on his face, and whose exploits had already filled the Indians with respect. He was one of the party who had come up the river and fastened the brass plate to the tree. The braves gave this man a peculiar name, but she afterwards learned that his own people called him John Smith and that this was not a peculiar name with them.

With the real onset of winter, the settlers grew more and more pinched for food. They succeeded in buying a few bushels of corn from a neighboring tribe, but not enough to tide them over. So Captain Smith decided to go deeper into the Indian country, as Powhatan speedily learned. Smith's party consisted of eight men, besides two Indian guides. They went by barge up the Chickahominy River right into the heart of Powhatan's domains. And hour by hour as they went forward they were jealously watched by picked men under Opecancanough.

After two days' progress through low, marshy country, the barge could not be taken farther. Leaving it, Smith pushed on ahead in a canoe with two men and the two guides, telling the others to stay on board until his return. They disobeyed his injunctions and it cost one of them his life. They went ashore and fell into an ambuscade. A sharp fight followed, and all the English escaped to the barge except the unfortunate fellow who was captured by the Indians. They tortured him, to find out other facts about the town, and then put him to death. The survivors made haste downstream to Jamestown, leaving Smith and the two others to their fate.

Smith's party meanwhile made its way some

miles upstream, and on a bit of rising ground went ashore to explore. He took one of the guides with him, leaving the other with his two companions. He had hardly passed out of ear-shot when the hidden foe again attacked, and the two men left behind were slain. Not knowing the fate of his comrades, Smith pushed on into the forest. It was desolate country now in the dead of winter, but if he felt any forebodings he gave no outward sign.

Suddenly the air seemed filled with whizzing arrows, and first one dark form and then another was seen darting from tree to tree. Instantly Smith was on the alert. Grasping his guide around the waist, he placed him in front of him-self as a sort of shield. Then he began to back away in the direction of the river. But the In-dians closed in from every direction. To add to his troubles, as he went backward he suddenly stepped into a bog and was mired. He had discharged his pistol, and as he had no chance to reload it he threw it away and held up his arms in token of surrender.

The scouts had evidently been instructed to take him alive, for they pulled him out of the mud and led him before Opecancanough. The latter gazed at the white chief with something like respect in his eye; while Smith beheld this fine-looking chief with secret admiration, but without quailing. The warrior had such an intelligent appearance, that Smith determined to impress him. He bethought himself of a pocket compass which he carried, and taking it out of his pocket he gravely handed it to the chief. The latter took it very gingerly and was amazed to see the needle flying about under the glass. He handed it to others of his braves, who could make nothing of it. Then Smith tried to explain it to them by signs, and even to give them a lesson in astronomy. The lecture proved too much for them, and was rudely interrupted by their seizing him and tying him up to a tree. They were about to make a living target out of him, when Opecancanough held up his hand, saying in a guttural voice which Smith could not understand but could guess at, "Release him. I would know something more of the white man's magic."

The prisoner was accordingly taken to the nearest village, and the vainglorious Opecancanough determined to make a great occasion of it. He went in advance with twenty warriors. Then came the prisoner with arms bound and guarded by three braves. Back of them came more warriors, all bedecked in feathers and paint. As they neared the village, they struck up a chant telling of their prowess and danced about, flourishing their weapons in Smith's face. All the women and children were drawn up on each

side of the trail leading into the village to welcome them. Then a great feast was spread, and
even Smith was invited to eat heartily and was
treated more as a guest of honor than an enemy.
For the crafty Opecancanough had changed his
plans. He was even then meditating an attack
upon Jamestown, and he thought he might get
some valuable information from his prisoner.
Further, he wanted to make another triumphal
entry into the head village where Powhatan re-
sided.

Smith was held at the first village for a week
or more. He quickly grasped many of their
words and signs, and learned of their campaign
against Jamestown. He must send his friends
warning in some way, he decided. The opportunity came, a few days later, when he was taken
into the wigwam of a man who had been wounded
and now lay at the point of death.

"You are a great medicine man," Smith was
told. "Save this man and we will spare your
life."

Smith saw that nothing could save the sufferer,
but dissembled. Here was a way to get a message through to Jamestown warning of the coming attack. He might also use it as a means
of impressing the savages with the power of the
white men's magic.

"I cannot heal him," he told them, "without

the proper medicine. Send some of your swift runners to Jamestown for the marvelous water there, and he will get well. Or let me go under guard and I will get it for you."

To the latter plan the wily Indians demurred, and they also wanted to know how the medicine could be obtained in his absence.

"I will make magic signs that the other white men can read, though many leagues away," replied Smith. And drawing out his notebook he extracted a page and wrote a message telling of his plight and asking them to give to the bearers a vial filled with well water. Then he warned them of the Indian plot and suggested that they take means of frightening the Indians by a display of cannon shot. The natives were used to the musketry by this time, but had not heard the big guns.

In three days the messengers returned, their eyes fairly bulging out at the wonders they had seen and heard. The white chief's magic was good; they had been given the healing waters just as he had foretold. Then a great roaring noise had burst forth as though the thunder-god had spoken. The ground rocked, and the limbs of trees coated with icicles had crashed to the ground. They—the messengers—had waited to see no more but had left that place of evil as fast as possible, and had not loitered on their return journey.

All this and much more the scouts related with many gesticulations. Captain Smith could not follow it all, but he caught enough to know that his warning had been delivered and the Indians were too much impressed to make an immediate attack.

However, his own troubles were by no means over. The sick man had died before the water could be brought back, and his nearest of kin again loudly clamored for the captive's life. Then they tried to impress him with their own magic. Several medicine men dressed and painted in black suddenly burst into the large wigwam where he sat with his hands tied behind him. With whoops and yells of frightful ferocity they danced about him, waving clubs and other weapons about his head. Then six more entered, three painted black, and three with red and white splotches. They danced about and shook rattles, after which they laid a circle of corn around the fire, and at every fifth grain they placed a small stick. A circle of cornmeal was also made on the floor.

By signs Smith asked what it was all about, and was told that they were trying to find out whether he were really a friend, or an enemy to be put to death. The meal stood for their country, the corn the bounds of the sea, and the sticks the white men. They could not, however, arrive at any conclusive answer.

Opecancanough was dissatisfied with his medicine men, and still more doubtful about putting Smith to death just to please them. He decided to stick to his original plan, and bring the white chief before Powhatan.

So through the snow-clad forests they took up their march again. All day they traveled and toward nightfall they reached the largest Indian town that Smith had yet seen. It was protected all about by a high palisade, whose only entrance was a narrow gateway.

As on the former occasion, Opecancanough made his approach as impressive as possible. Tom-toms apprised the inhabitants that he was on his way, and soon the entire village was lined up along the trail to greet him. Warriors in gay paint and feathers preceded and followed the prisoner, who on his part held his head erect and gazed without fear at the multitude.

In the center of the town was a large council house which was now thronged with warriors. There must have been two hundred of them. In the midst a large fire was burning which at times sent clouds of smoke around the room. At the far end of the council chamber was a raised dais thickly strewn with the fine pelts of animals, and on a sort of throne sat the powerful head-chief of all this country, Powhatan. Smith averred afterwards that he had stood before royalty and nobility in many lands, but had never seen one who exceeded this potentate in majesty and dignity. He wore a long robe of raccoon skins, and a strand of pearls around his neck. His sixty years or more sat lightly upon him, as he was muscular and well proportioned, with little gray in his hair.

Seated at his feet was a young girl who gazed wide-eyed at this stranger about whom she had heard so many tales. It was Pocahontas, the favorite daughter of the old chief.

Then ensued a powwow, which was becoming familiar to the prisoner. Powhatan in a deep rich voice began to question him. Whence came he? What was his purpose in the Indian's country? And many more.

"I come many and many moons' journey from across the Great Waters," answered Smith. "Our ship, which you call the big canoe, goes forward with the winds of heaven and not by the hand of man. So we are protected by the Great Spirit. He it was who drove us by these winds into your goodly harbor. So we landed, and I have taken the first opportunity to come and pay my respects to your all-powerful self."

This and other flowery speeches did he address

to Powhatan who, if he were gratified or impressed, did not show it. The little girl, however, drank in every word eagerly. This white man with the big beard was as a god to her.

At a sign from the ruler, women brought a platter of meat and set it before Smith, who welcomed it, as the long march had made him feel famished. While he ate, Powhatan and his brother, Opecancanough, conferred long and earnestly about the prisoner. Smith knew they were deciding his fate but did not let that fact destroy his appetite.

Then Powhatan began to speak. He told of his power, and the extent of his dominions. From the waters of the sea far back into the unknown mountains of the west his possessions ran. This was the domain of the Indians, over whom he was lord and king. How, then, did the paleface dare to land on his shores and even build towns without his permission?

Smith answered boast with boast. He served a king who was far more powerful—one who sent ships into every sea. They had weapons of fire and thunder which struck down all who opposed them. Yet his king would be a friend and brother to Powhatan, if he so wished.

"Soon," he ended unwisely, "he will send more and more of these winged boats to your shores."

By the stir which went around the hall and

the ugly scowls which greeted him, Smith knew that he had said the wrong thing. Angry voices were raised here and there, and protests against allowing this white boaster to live. "Kill him, and kill every other paleface who trespasses on our land," they said. "Thus only shall we go and come as our fathers did."

Powhatan himself remained silent during this impassioned debate. At last he raised his hand for silence, and made a wide sweeping motion. This was greeted with yells of delight, and two huge warriors went outside, soon returning and bearing a large stone between them. This was placed on the ground, and other men entered with heavy war clubs. Smith now saw that he had been condemned to death, but that he would not be tortured. It would be a quick and merciful end, as the first blow would render him unconscious.

Disdaining to plead for mercy or otherwise show the white feather, he went without protest to the stone, stretched himself out and placed his head upon it. One of the braves lifted his club high in the air, but before it could descend a piercing shriek was heard, and the little Pocahontas sprang forward and shielded the victim with her own body. With extended arms she knelt there and turned her eyes upon her father.

"He shall not die! Spare him!" she cried.

In every Indian's soul there is a sense of the dramatic. This unexpected interference, far from displeasing the throng, secretly pleased them. The white prisoner could be slain any time—and perhaps the next time by torture. Powhatan also wavered. This man might be of far more service to them alive than dead. And to grant a boon to his favored child pleased him. He waved his arm.

"Release him," he said. "I give him to Pocahontas. He shall be her slave until I require him again."

Pocahontas herself aided in loosing the captive's bonds with eager hands. He smiled his thanks to her, and then slowly got to his feet and stood again before the king.

"You owe your life to her," said Powhatan. "Do as she bids you, until I send for you again."

Pocahontas took his hand and led him away between the lines of frowning braves. For the time being he was safe.

The days that followed were strange ones to the doughty captain, but he played the role of servant to a small, pampered Indian maiden very gallantly. He made wonderful toys and dolls for her, whittling them out with his trusty jack-knife. He showed her the compass and—as they learned words of each other's tongue—he told her about the boys and girls living beyond the seas.

He showed her a few beads which still happened to be in his pocket, and promised her a whole handful of them if she would visit Jamestown some day with him. From time to time, indeed, he mentioned Jamestown with its marvels, in the hope that Powhatan might perchance send him there. For his heart was filled with foreboding about the fate of the colonists.

Pocahontas doubtless told her father about the proposed trip to the settlement, and he in turn showed an interest in the venture. He particularly longed to have one or two of those mighty guns which roared like thunder and shattered the limbs of trees. If he but possessed these, he reasoned, he would be the most powerful chief who had ever lived.

Powhatan held more than one talk with his unwilling guest, and gradually Smith began to read his mind. He finally said that he would send Smith back under guard and would make a treaty with his people—in return for two of the cannon, some knives, and other gifts. To this, we may be sure, Smith readily agreed. Pocahontas likewise was delighted at the prospect, and promised that she would come a few days later and bring baskets of food.

And thus at last Captain John Smith got back to Jamestown. He had been gone nearly five weeks, and the others had given him up for dead.

They themselves were in a dreadful plight; their food was almost entirely gone, and many were sick of scurvy and want. The leaders, in fact, were preparing to desert in the one small remaining ship and leave the rest to their fate.

Smith's quick eye took in the situation at a glance. He reproached the faint-hearted ones, and bade all the others take heart again. He had made a treaty with Powhatan, and food was even then on its way. Then he showed his Indian guards around the fort, gave them knives and other presents, and finally led them to the two culverins which he had promised the sachem.

"There are the two great guns for Powhatan," he said. "They are yours; take them."

The natives grunted and stooped to lift them —but they grunted again, in a different fashion when they found they couldn't budge them. Again and again they tried, but had to give over in disgust, just as Smith had foreseen.

On the next day, true to her word, Pocahontas came into Jamestown, and with her a long line of women carrying corn, venison, and other much-needed food. They were like angels from heaven in the sight of the suffering colonists. Pocahontas darted from place to place, like any other eager child, and asked her white captain a thousand questions. And how delighted was she, on departing, to receive a bead necklace, a bit of bright cloth, and many other little treasures. This was only one of many such visits paid by Pocahontas to the town, and never did she come empty-handed. She was indeed a ministering angel to them, and her father for her sake maintained his treaty of peace and withheld his tribes.

With the coming of spring things looked brighter for the colonists. The supplies brought in by the Indians tided them through, and another shipload of men and material had arrived from England. More ground was tilled, and soon fresh vegetables and fruits made their welcome appearance. The colonists, however, did not take warning from the bitter lesson of the preceding winter and lay up all possible provisions. Instead, they feasted each day on the fat of the land and even ate up the ship's stores. Many of the new colonists, in fact, were "gentlemen born" who strutted about in velvets and expected others to wait upon them; while some were tradesmen, such as goldsmiths and tailors, who knew little and cared less about farming.

Smith was in despair at the way things were going on. He served as governor for a time, but his insistence that every man should work made him unpopular.

With the approach of another winter his worst fears were realized. Again the settlers ran short of food. The Indians held them in open con-

tempt at this second crisis. The palefaces must
be poor men indeed not to be able to make a living off the land. Smith went again to trade with
Powhatan, but the latter, while outwardly
friendly, was disposed to make a sharp bargain.
In particular he wanted some of the white men's
guns—a thing that the captain was loath to grant
him.

Smith made several trips of trade and explora-
tion among the Virginia tribes that year. Then
he met with a severe accident. A bag of gun-
powder exploded in his boat, burning him ter-
ribly. While still a sick man he was sent back
to England by the others, who were glad to get
rid of the "trouble-maker," and the tribes of Virginia saw him no more.

However, the settlers soon had cause to regret
their action. With the doughty captain gone,
the Indians again became troublesome. Pocahontas was one of the few who remained loyal,
and through her timely warning, more than one
threatened attack was averted. Powhatan was
no longer to be trusted, although outwardly
friendly. On one occasion a company of thirty
men sent to trade with him fell into an ambuscade, and only two escaped to reach Jamestown.
Whether all the rest were slain or merely carried
into captivity, no one ever heard.

The succeeding winter was so terrible in its

suffering that it was known ever after as the "Starving Time." The men were reduced to digging up frozen roots and gnawing them. They even ate rats and dogs. By spring only a handful remained alive. Then came more ships and supplies from England, and the colony at last survived.

For some months nothing was heard directly from Powhatan, and Pocahontas came no more to the town. Rumor had it that the chief had removed his headquarters still farther west so as to get as far away from the English as possible. Meanwhile the petty depredations of the Indians continued. It was not safe to leave anything lying about, especially swords, knives, or guns. Nor was it safe for a white man to venture far in the forest.

Some colonists had been made prisoners by the Indians, and a shrewd move was resolved upon. If a few of the natives could be seized and held as hostages, the white men might be ransomed and a stop could be put to the thievery. The only difficulty was in laying their hands upon the Indians, who came no more boldly into camp. The governor and his council debated the matter for some time, and finally decided to seize one person—Pocahontas herself. It was a perfidious act in view of the many kindnesses which she had shown them, but they argued that no harm should

befall her, and that Powhatan would not dare
to make trouble, if she were in their hands.

The plot was carried out successfully. The
girl was lured on shipboard and brought down
to Jamestown, despite her tears and entreaties.
Captain Argall, her captor, treated her with
courtesy and respect, and at last made her understand why she was held. In time she became
reconciled to the white men's way, and she was a
general favorite. She learned to speak English
and dress in English clothes, and finally was baptized in the little church at Jamestown.

As for Powhatan he was in a towering rage,
and for several weeks would not treat with the
English at all. When he at last became convinced that no harm was intended to his
daughter, he gradually renewed the treaty and
sent back some prisoners. But Pocahontas came
no more into his lodges.

It was at the time of her baptism that the
English learned with surprise that her real name
was not Pocahontas. They had christened her
Rebecca, and as the Lady Rebecca she was later
known in England. But she averred that her
name was Matoaka. Powhatan admitted that
this was so, and when asked why she was not
called thus, he answered: "I feared to tell her
real name to the white men lest they cast an evil
spell upon her."

Pocahontas—as we must still call her—grew up into womanhood in the colony, loved and respected by all. In particular one young tobacco planter, an Englishman of good family, was devoted to her. John Rolfe finally sought her hand in marriage. Powhatan gave his consent, but would not attend the ceremony in person. He never came near Jamestown, as he seemed to think it beneath his dignity, but he sent his brother and other warriors all decked in their finest.

This marriage, celebrated in the old church, was the most important event of its kind for many years. Pocahontas looked every inch a princess, and Sir Thomas Dale, the governor, who attended with all the dignitaries of church and state, gave her away to the happy groom. The little brick church with its pews of cedar, its walnut pulpit and fan-shaped windows, was a bower of roses on that momentous day.

The young couple sailed for England on their honeymoon, a plan to which Powhatan also gave his consent.

"Go," he said, "and come back to tell me about the English king and the land across the sea. For I would know more concerning the white man's ways."

Pocahontas, likewise, was delighted. Now, perhaps, she could see again her childhood's hero,

Captain John Smith—one whom she had never ceased to miss.

When the party had arrived in London, the Lady Rebecca was showered with honors such as were accorded to royalty. The English looked upon her as the daughter of an emperor, and some questioned the presumption of plain John Rolfe in marrying a princess. Pocahontas, however, bore her new honors modestly and created a favorable impression by her charm of manner. She was presented at court and entertained by royalty.

Always on entering a room her bright eyes glanced around the throng in search of one familiar face; and the first question she had asked on reaching England was: "Is Captain John Smith still alive?"

Some said that he was dead; others, that he had gone on new travels and adventures, for his was a roving spirit not content with the idleness of civilization. He it was who explored the coast of New England and paved the way for the coming of the Pilgrim Fathers to Plymouth. Then they said he had gone to France where, in the wars, he had been taken prisoner. Some time later there came the joyful word to her that he was alive and would shortly be in London.

At one of the court receptions her dark eyes found him at last; a grizzled veteran, yet bearing his years stoutly. She knew him at once, and despite the courtiers and ladies standing about in their velvets, silks, and laces, she rushed up to him with arms outstretched, crying "My father!"

Although he knew who it was, he had difficulty in recognizing in this stately young woman dressed in the height of fashion, the simple child of the Virginia backwoods. This was a gracious lady of flawless speech and manners who would grace any court.

Mindful of the rigors of court etiquette, he contented himself with lifting her hand respectfully and kissing it.

"Welcome to England," he said, while his face lighted up to express more than the formal words.

"My father!" she exclaimed again.

"Nay, not so," he protested gently. "I dare not allow that title, for you are a king's daughter, and I am only plain John Smith."

She looked at him steadily.

"Dare not?" she repeated. "Captain Smith *dare* not? That is not *my* captain! I tell you, I *will* call you father!"

And—needless to say—she did.

Many a talk did the old friends have together. And from John Rolfe the captain learned much of the later history of his colony.

With this happy reunion we would like to close

the chronicle of Pocahontas, but stern history gives us the final scene. She began to weary of the round of social life and to pine for her beloved Virginia. A son was born to her, and her health failed. She caught a severe cold which the London fogs aggravated. In alarm her husband planned a speedy return to Virginia. Captain Argall,—the same who had made her a prisoner some years before—was in harbor preparing to sail. But before he weighed anchor, she had breathed her last. As the *George,* his ship, put to sea her body was carried into the church at Gravesend, where a funeral service was read.

Rolfe and his little son sailed alone. The son lived to be the founder of one of the most famous families in the colony that his mother had befriended.

When the *George* dropped anchor in Jamestown harbor, and Rolfe came ashore alone, more than one face was wet with the tears of honest sympathy, as his neighbors silently shook him by the hand. The bell in the square church tower tolled, and another solemn service was held for the girl who had lately gone forth as a bride.

"She was our patron saint," they said. And they spoke truly.

CHAPTER THREE

OPECANCANOUGH, THE SCOURGE OF VIRGINIA

"THE paleface comes farther and farther into our lands. It is time for us to strike!"

Thus spake the chief, Opecancanough, to his braves as they sat around the council fire. The time was the year 1618. According to the white man's reckoning the settlement at Jamestown was now eleven years old, and in those eleven years the Indians had seen, with increasing uneasiness, the spread of the colony far inland. It was no longer a handful of men living from hand to mouth and begging corn of the natives in the wintertime; it was a growing and prosperous colony.

The chief reason for its prosperity lay in one product—tobacco. The settlers had learned the use of this plant from the natives and had introduced it into England, where smoking and snufftaking became the rage. The Indians themselves had not cultivated the plant in large crops, but had only little patches to supply their own needs. Left to itself, it grew wild.

John Rolfe, the husband of Pocahontas, was one of the first to see its commercial possibilities. One day as he bartered with the Indians for some of their tobacco, he thought, "If the natives can grow this weed to profit, why cannot I?" The next time he was in one of their villages he observed carefully how it was cultivated and obtained some of the seed. He began in a small way on his own land and was so successful that he in turn began selling it to his neighbors. Soon others and still others caught the "tobacco fever" and planted more and more land in it, almost to the exclusion of necessary crops. Shiploads were sent to the home country where they fetched a fancy price. So prosperous did the trade become in a few years that it marked the turning of the tide for Virginia. It had become not only self-supporting but a paying colony, and hundreds of new settlers were attracted. In the harbor might often be seen several vessels at once, and flying various flags.

All this had the Indians seen, and—while the white men exulted—they scowled. They saw the ever-growing tobacco plantations reaching out into the forests. Trees were felled and the wild game scurried farther into the fastnesses.

"The white man is a fool," said Opecancanough contemptuously. "He makes tobacco his god. He neglects corn for his belly to get tobacco for his nose. He even grows it in the streets of his villages, and buys his wives with it!"

Which was true. Tobacco had become the medium of exchange. Everything else was measured by it; and when a shipload of prospective brides had been sent over from England, to make up for the dearth of womenfolk in the colony, the husbands-to-be had to pay their passage in so-and-so-many hogsheads of tobacco before the bans were declared.

Another warrior then spoke up. "Yes," he said, "tobacco is the white man's god. As he watches its leaves sprouting out of the ground, he does not see the war omens in the sky. An eagle might fly past, its talons filled with arrows, but he would see it not. You, O mighty Opecancanough,"—he ended flatteringly—"are that eagle."

The chief smiled at this compliment but kept silent for others to speak. He saw his long-laid plans coming to a head. He had long coveted the power of the great Powhatan, and now the latter had gone at last to the Happy Hunting Grounds. Although the lordship had fallen to an older son, Opecancanough had found means to thrust him aside and take the head-chiefship. For many moons now he had gone from tribe to tribe cementing them to himself through their common fear of the constantly encroaching English.

"He speaks truth," they agreed. "We must fight the palefaces and drive them out; else will we be their slaves."

They had reason for their fears. The English had become so strong along the Tidewater that they ceased to regard the Indians. What land they desired they took. The natives might like it or not.

The Indians who lived nearest to the settlements had ceased to protest at the changed condition of affairs. They went back and forth freely on terms of peace and friendliness. They were given food by the settlers' wives, and perhaps paused to pinch the cheeks of the laughing boys and girls playing in the lanes. Some were employed on the plantations, but they did not like to work and made poor servants. The planters thereupon began to buy Negro slaves brought from Africa by thrifty Dutch traders.

Little by little the Indians obtained guns and learned to handle them quite as proficiently as their bows. The governor, Yeardley, had an Indian manservant who went regularly into the woods and fields to hunt game for him. However, so many years had passed by in peace that the English ceased to look upon their Indian neighbors as possible enemies. No guards were maintained and the palisades and forts were suffered to rot away. Everyone was too busy cultivating tobacco.

Four years passed by after Powhatan was gathered to his fathers, and still no cloud came to disturb the peaceful sky. Opecancanough was not seen near the settlements and no word came from him. Indeed, the busy planters gave scarcely a thought to any of the Indians; and the wily chief chose a waiting game.

Nemattanow, the flatterer, however, was not so circumspect. He was a young, vainglorious brave whom the English laughingly called "Jack of the Feather," as he always went strutting about with one eagle's feather sticking straight up out of his scalp-lock. Fired by Opecancanough's eloquence, he took it upon himself to stir up his people to a sense of their wrongs. He openly boasted that no bullet could hurt him. This idle boast reached the ears of his white neighbors, who only smiled the more when they saw him parading by.

One morning Nemattanow lost his head and started out on his own private warpath. He had seen at the home of a planter named Morgan some brightly shining trinkets which made his palms itch covetously. Not having a chance to take them, he went out into the field where Morgan was at work and told him of his desires. The

planter started with him to the house to see about
a trade, but on the way Nemattanow turned
upon him, killed him without warning, and then
went to the house alone and took the things he
had coveted.

Another white man had seen the attack and
hastened after the marauder. In the fight that
ensued the Indian in turn was slain.

Before another morning's sun, swift-footed
runners brought to Opecancanough's ears the
story of this deed. His brow darkened, his fists
clenched, but presently he said to his messenger
in smooth tones: "Go to the governor and tell
him that the sky may fall sooner than Opecancanough will break the peace of his fathers."

When other braves at the council growled sullenly at this, he turned upon them with a stern
"Not yet!"

Only a few days after this a party of Englishmen out hunting got lost in the woods. When
the fact was gleefully reported to the chief, he
sent two of his guides to conduct them safely
home and with further messages of friendship to
the governor.

And thus followed the early days of spring in
this direful year, 1622, with the sky gleaming
peaceful overhead, and the prospects of yet
greater crops. With the time for the clearing
and plowing of the soil, the colonists found much

work to do. From early sun-up to late into the twilight they toiled, while the no less busy housewives went about their many chores at home. Here and there Indians might be seen stalking about in twos and threes, sometimes pausing to talk to the children, or ask food, as was their custom, since they were the only idlers in this industrious community, but they were a familiar sight and elicited no second glance.

The scene on March the 22nd was like that of the preceding days, the sun shining brightly on a busy, contented colony reaching many miles up and down the Virginia coast. Then it was, without warning, that the wily Opecancanough struck—not merely in one spot but in many at once; for he planned nothing less than the entire extermination of the hated white people.

The Indians, who but a moment before had been smiling and talking with some settler's family, suddenly drew forth tomahawks and clubs and struck down the defenseless women and children without mercy. The men rushing in from the fields were slain before they could lay hands upon their weapons. Here, there, and everywhere the once harmless Indians rushed, yelling and screeching like fiends. The sight of blood had let loose the long-pent-up hatred of the white man and they were like devils. None was spared, young or old, of either sex. They took no prisoners. Houses were fired, and soon a pall of smoke hung over the land like a forest fire.

The attack had come so unexpectedly that the white men were at a great disadvantage. They fought with the energy of despair, using fence rails, hoes, or any other weapon they could lay their hands upon. In the little settlement of Falling Creek, near what was later Richmond, only two out of twenty-four persons escaped. They were children who had been out in the field and hid themselves until the fire and carnage passed them by.

Jamestown was saved only by the narrowest of margins—the personal fidelity of one Indian lad. He was the servant of a farmer named Pace, but had always been treated with the greatest kindness, more like a son than a servant. On the night before the massacre, the boy's older brother had come to him secretly and told him it was his job to slay his employer. The boy agreed but during the night his heart failed him. He crept instead into his master's bedroom before dawn and warned him of the impending danger. At first, Pace could not believe the story, so wild and fantastic it sounded, but the boy was so in earnest in his entreaties that at last he took alarm. Saddling his swiftest horse, he galloped down to Jamestown, a few miles away, and aroused the sleeping citizens. When the vanguard of Indians arrived, they found the colonists grimly awaiting them.

Despite the suddenness of Opecancanough's attack, and its widespread character, the chief did not succeed in blotting out the colony. Instead, he encountered such unexpected but determined resistance that by the end of that gory day his warriors were in retreat. But they left behind them the mangled bodies of three hundred and forty-seven victims—a terrible toll upon the little colony. Six members of the governor's own council were slain, and a score of little settlements reduced to smoking ruins. Jamestown would have shared a like fate, but for Pace's timely warning. For a hundred miles along the Virginia coast, yesterday smiling and happy, the sun went down on desolated homes and the sight of men with grim or grief-stricken faces searching for their loved ones.

With the dawning of another day the tables were turned. The Indians were in full retreat and the white men, hastily formed into companies, were on their trail. No time was to be lost if they were to be brought to retribution, as once lost in the dense forests to the west they were safe. Hard and fast marched the volunteer soldiers, leaving scarcely enough men back in the colony to bury the dead, but this was no day of

halfway measures. The settlers in turn thirsted
for blood and were quite as savage as the natives.

By twos and threes they overhauled the scattered Indians, and they slew them without mercy.
It was an eye for an eye, and a tooth for a tooth.
The Indians nowhere made a determined stand
but, true to their methods of warfare, after having once struck they scattered. It was every man
for himself.

Opecancanough soon learned the difference between his type of warfare and that of the hated
paleface. Day by day the chase continued. Farther and farther back his bands were driven, paying a heavy toll as they went. The few Indian
villages encountered were utterly destroyed, with
their food supplies, and if any women or children
were luckless enough to be left behind, they met
the same fate that had befallen the settlers'
families.

When the chief and his harried followers
finally came together in the mountains many
miles from the settlements they were weary, hag-
gard, and vengeful. They had lost many of their
best men, and they knew that their power was
broken. They realized that, instead of being allowed to come and go freely as in the past, they
would live like hunted animals. However, Opecancanough still drew himself up proudly and
looked about the circle of his braves.

"The sun has gone down in blood," he said, "and the eagle screams over the ashes of many homes. The paleface who disdained us yesterday fears us to-day. Let us never yield!"

At the governor's council in Jamestown the white men took similar stock of the situation. The colony had suffered a terrible blow which would stay its progress for many years, but there must be no retreat.

"It is all very well to say 'no retreat,'" said one planter bitterly; "but what can we do? We can no longer extend our tobacco fields out into the edges of the forest, for every tree may conceal a lurking foe. And without our tobacco our prosperity is gone."

"Nathless, we must live together more closely in the stockaded towns," replied the governor. "Our very existence as a colony is at stake now."

The planters gloomily agreed that he was right, and many an estate was abandoned to grow up again in weeds, while the owner went to live in the towns along the river and shore. Trade dropped off rapidly, and the ships no longer plied busily back and forth. Worst of all, an epidemic sprang up that summer, due to poor water and crowded living conditions. The affairs of Virginia had again reached a low ebb.

When word was brought to the wily chief, he grunted his satisfaction. "The serpent can strike

as deadly a blow as the bear," he said. "Let
there be no peace with the white intruders."

As the months passed by, however, he saw the
hated colony taking a firmer and firmer hold.
More ships came, and the palisades were again
pushed farther and farther to enclose choice
lands in the west. The Indians were compelled
to make their peace, although they were never
again fully trusted. The planters in the fields
always kept their weapons handy.

A new governor came over from England, who
seemed to be a great chief indeed as he was driven
about in his fine coach, and appeared upon the
streets dressed in velvets and laces. He was the
famous Sir William Berkeley, full of the king's
importance, and giving scant heed to Indian
claims. In his eyes all the domains belonged
to the king of England, and the natives could be
dealt with only as inferiors. When any of the
braves came to his council chamber or visited him
on his estate, he received them graciously enough,
but gave them to understand that the sovereign
across the seas was their father, and held them
in the hollow of his hand.

Year by year sped by thus, in outward peace,
but with inner discontent on the part of the Indians. They watched their choicest hunting
grounds become cleared for the great tobacco
plantations. They saw Negro slaves toiling in

the fields. They beheld fine ladies and gentlemen riding by on horseback or in carriages enjoying all this land that they had held as their
own. Within the next twenty years, indeed, Virginia had grown so prosperous that its people
were concerned with the affairs of trade and
fashion, and had wellnigh forgotten the terrible
massacre of 1622.

Not so, Opecancanough. Back in his wilderness home he still nursed his hatred against the
intruders, and dreamed of a day when they
should be driven out, and his land restored to
his people. He was now nearly a hundred years
old, for it had been many a long moon since he
had first captured Captain Smith in the forest.
It is said his eyelids were so weak that they had
to be lifted by someone else, to enable him to see.
His wasted form, once so erect and muscular,
must be carried on a litter. But his indomitable
spirit was unbroken, and he was still looked up
to as the head-chief, the successor of the great
Powhatan.

As his scouts came to him, complaining that
the Indians were being crowded more and more
to the west, and that the white men, even when
they made a treaty, did not abide by it, the old
man's eyes flashed with renewed fire. In a
hoarse but stern voice he bade his followers make
a last stand.

"Will ye give up the lands of your fathers like whipped dogs?" he cried. "I am old, but if you will carry me into battle, I will show you how to strike!"

His fiery speech again kindled them, and from far and near the warriors came secretly to his council. There plans were laid for another surprise attack such as had been made twenty years before. The early days of spring were again chosen, when the English would be widely scattered around their fields preparing for another year's crop.

The blow this time fell upon the outlying settlements near Pamunkey and to the south of James River. At early dawn on an April day in 1644, the Indians might have been seen filing through the woods, and at their head was a rude litter borne by four men. It was Opecancanough going again on the warpath. As he neared the settlement he sniffed the air excitedly. His keen scent told him what his eye could not see. He told his men to spread out and strike as widely as possible, before the households were astir.

"Strike and spare none!" he harangued. "Burn their houses! Kill every one you meet. The number of scalplocks you bring back proves how great a warrior you are."

This was music in the ears of the younger braves, who had been complaining that the days of peace had kept them from obtaining any scalps, and without these trophies the Indian maidens would not look at them.

Burning to distinguish themselves, the braves scattered into little groups and attacked the defenseless plantations and hamlets. Again as their fathers had done, they dashed out into the open screeching like fiends and carrying flame and death before them. Soon their cries were met by the shrill screaming of their helpless victims, or the hoarse cries of men. Shots resounded on every side, and then to the old chief's dilated nostrils came the welcome, pungent odor of smoke. It was the great day of vengeance, of which he had dreamed, come at last.

But for the white men it was another terrible day of distress and bloodshed. The slaughter almost rivalled that of the other direful massacre of which they had so often heard. Three hundred men, women, and children were slain before the settlers could make headway against the yelling Indian hordes. Here and there pitched battles ensued between small groups of whites and natives. No quarter was expected, and none was shown.

Toward nightfall the Indians were again in retreat. They had struck their blow, now they sought shelter in the woods. Opecancanough tried to rally them for renewed attack, but the

Indian braves had no stomach for continuous fighting. He railed and stormed as his litter men carried him back into the wilderness.

As for Sir William Berkeley, his rage knew no bounds when he heard of this new attack. It was an insult to the king's majesty as well as a fresh setback to the colony. The natives must be stamped out like so much vermin. He organized a band of soldiers, nearly all of whom were expert shots, and trained woodsmen, to follow hard upon the Indians and give them no rest day or night. They were to be slain on sight. Opecancanough, their leader, however, must be captured—if not alive, then dead. Sir William had heard many tales of this old chieftain, and would see him with his own eyes.

Swift and bloody retribution was meted out to the fleeing followers of Opecancanough, and his litter-carriers could not make fast progress through the woods. Before many days he was captured and brought at last into Jamestown, the town that he had scorned for a lifetime to visit. Sir William looked down from the portico of the statehouse while the old chieftain was carried along. Here was the ancient trouble-maker brought to bay at last.

The captive was left on view in the market-place, where the crowd jostled about in the attempt to get a good look at him. He heard the commotion, and asked a boy who attended him to lift up his eyelids so that he could see. A scornful gleam replaced the dimness of his vision as he glimpsed the gaping throng.

"Bear this message to your governor," he said to one of his guards. "Tell him that if it had been my fortune to take Sir William Berkeley prisoner, I would have disdained to make a show of him!"

Not long, however, was Opecancanough's pride to suffer. One of his guards who, perchance, had lost someone of his own family in the massacre, bent on revenge, shot the helpless prisoner in the back. He died soon after, and, it is said, was buried in the churchyard near the end of the little peninsula whereon Jamestown stood. In years to come, the waters encroached more and more upon the shore line and—long after the town itself was abandoned—his bones were swept out into the tide. Even in death he could not rest in peace, but doubtless his spirit preferred this to consorting with his enemies, whom he had fought his life long.

Thus passed the first great scourge of the Virginia colony—Opecancanough, the irreconcilable.

CHAPTER FOUR

SQUANTO, THE FRIEND OF THE PILGRIMS

"WELCOME, Englishmen!"

The persons greeted started back in astonishment. The man who had uttered these words was a naked Indian, save for a strip of leather ornamented with a deep fringe, although it was a chilly March day in New England. Yet he had greeted them in their native English tongue. While they stared at him, he said again:

"Welcome, Englishmen!"

One can picture their surprise when the attendant circumstances are understood. The Pilgrims, a band of colonists, had come to the coast of what is now Massachusetts in the dead of winter, at the end of the year 1620. They had landed at Plymouth and begun a town there, but in the rigors of a cold and desolate land it had been a hard struggle. They had seen but few Indians, as a pestilence had carried off nearly all the inhabitants along the coast only a few months before they landed. The ones they had seen had run away in alarm. Now an Indian

stepped boldly from the thicket and, coming up
to the guards posted on the hilltop overlooking
the village, had said in the English tongue,
"Welcome!"

It was enough to give them a shock of surprise.

Regaining their wits, the guards answered him,
and then deciding that the head men should be
the first to question him, they bade him follow
them. This he did willingly enough, and with
every evidence of friendliness. Down the single
long street of the straggling village they went,
and past the score or more log huts, until they
came to the square meeting-house, which also
served as a council chamber.

A little squad of soldiers under the bold Miles
Standish was on guard, and at the table sat Ed-
ward Winslow, William Brewster, young William Bradford, and other leaders. They looked
up gravely as the tall, naked Indian stalked in.

"How!" he said, giving them an Indian salute.
Then he added the single word, "Peace!"

The Englishmen glanced at him and then at
each other. With one accord they rose and answered his greeting. "We are friends," they
said.

"My name Samoset," he continued. "I speak
the English as you, I have met the palefaces
under other suns."

Then he told them of meeting with fishermen

on the coast to the north of them (what is now
Maine) and how he had learned to speak their
language. While he answered their questions,
the time for the noon meal came, and he did not
need an urgent invitation for—like many Indians
they were to meet with later—he was hungry.
He ate nearly as much as three men, then a full
stomach still further loosed his tongue. He told
them of the terrible disease which had blotted
out the Indian villages for miles along the coast.
He said that he belonged to the tribe of Wampanoags, who had escaped the plague and were
neighbors of the colonists. Their chief, Massasoit, would pay them a visit shortly.

"Why do the Indians run away from us?" he
was asked.

"Because, some moons ago, another party of
palefaces came in their great canoe with wings.
Our men were friends with them and gave them
food and the skins of animals. But they laid
harsh hands upon us, and some they carried away
with them across the great waters."

What Samoset said was true. One of the first
English ships which touched at Cape Cod, before
the coming of the Pilgrims, had kidnapped some
of the natives and sold them into slavery. One
of these—as Samoset related—was a boy of
about twelve summers, named Squanto. The
voyage across to England and the scenes he wit-

nessed must have been strange indeed to this child of the wilderness. He was not mistreated, but was made to work with tools that were unlike any he knew. He learned the language and the ways of the English. Best of all, he won the friendship of a kind-hearted man, who ransomed him and sent him back to his own land on a trading vessel. Now Squanto was a young brave, but he had not forgotten the English speech he had learned.

All this Samoset told in halting sentences, accompanied by many gestures. "I think he like see you," he ended. "I bring him."

As night drew on, Samoset made no move to leave the village. He was having too good a time, and his nose told him that something was in the pot stewing over the great fire. They fed him again, and seeing that he intended to pass the night with them, they made the best of it. But they posted a guard before the house where he slept, to prevent surprise. The next morning after breakfast, he departed with renewed protestations of friendship and soon was lost to view in the forest.

A day or two later, true to his promise, he came again, and with him was a younger Indian just grown who looked about him with lively interest. It was Squanto, the boy who had been taken across the seas and learned something of the paleface way of living.

"Me, Squanto," he said smiling. "I come to your village to live with you, to be friends."

Captain Miles Standish looked him over critically. He saw a well-set-up young brave of more than ordinary intelligence. He could be useful to them as an interpreter and go-between, and so the captain told Bradford and the others.

"You shall be our chief scout," the soldier told him; "and so long as you talk straight, you will find shelter and food with us. But what Squanto's eye sees his tongue must tell."

"Squanto's tongue is not forked like the snake's. He will talk straight to his white friends."

This assertion of the young brave he lived up to. He dealt fairly with the colonists. Only once in the succeeding months was his veracity questioned, and that may not have been his fault. He was of the highest service to the struggling and hard-pressed Pilgrims. They had come to a strange land in the midst of winter, their supplies were running low, and they had lost many of their number through privation and sickness. They did not know the temper of the natives round about them, and each morning from their lookout on the hill they had scanned the surrounding country with anxious eyes. To have first one and then another friendly Indian come to them—and, best of all, speaking English, was a Godsend indeed.

Squanto told them readily about the various tribes that lived nearest to them, and of the country. He told them of the fierce Narragansetts who lived to the south, and of his own people, the Wampanoags.

"Massasoit, our big chief, he coming see you soon," he announced.

"How soon?" asked Standish, not knowing whether Massasoit came as a friend or an enemy.

"Four, five sunrises—what you say, a week," replied the scout.

The truth of this statement was soon proved when, one morning, a considerable party of Indians was seen emerging from the fringe of forest. At their head came a dignified, elderly warrior, whom Squanto identified as Massasoit. Straight up to the stockade they marched, giving no indication as to whether their visit was peaceful or otherwise. Captain Standish was taking no chances.

"Go out to Massasoit," he said, "and tell him he cannot enter until we parley."

Squanto went, and they saw him talking and gesticulating with the chief, who answered by grunts and nods. Soon he came back.

"The great chief comes as a friend and would smoke the pipe of peace with you," he reported.

"Tell him that our lodge is small, although our hearts are large," replied the captain. "He and twenty of his men may enter, but in token of friendship they are to leave their weapons outside."

This also Squanto told the chief and after making two or three trips back and forth, the gates were thrown open to Massasoit and twenty of his braves. Meanwhile, Standish had not been idle in his preparations. The little settlement must make a brave show. Just as the chief wrapped in his cloak and wearing an eagle's feather stalked through the gate, his ears were assailed by strange sounds. The deep, rapid roll of a drum was followed by the shrill blast of a bugle, and this in turn by a deafening report of six muskets. All were in his honor, but despite himself his knees shook and the whites of his eyes showed. Captain Standish held out his hand reassuringly.

"Tell him," he said to Squanto, "that his white brother greets him with the salute of kings."

Suspecting that the chief's heart might be won through his stomach, Standish had a feast made ready from the scanty supplies still left in the garrison, and they were all seated cross-legged before a roaring fire, eating potlatch and licking their fingers appreciatively. After they had eaten their fill—and doubtless to the envy of the hungry warriors left on the outside of the stockade—they continued to sit contentedly around the fire, the white men mingling freely with the Indians.

At a signal from the chief, young Squanto filled a calumet or peace pipe, with tobacco leaf, lighted it from a glowing coal which he caught up dexterously with his bare hands, and passed it to Massasoit. He took a few puffs and handed it to Standish.

"It is the pipe of peace," Squanto said rapidly, not knowing how much of the Indian ways his white friends understood. The captain bowed gravely—he already knew of this custom—and the pledge of amity passed from one to another until it had completed the circle. Then the old chief began to speak, stopping every few words for Squanto to translate.

"Our white brothers now know our thoughts," he said. "The smoke of the calumet is like the breath of the Great Spirit coming into all our hearts with the same message. The Wampanoags come to their white brothers with open hands and hearts. Our land is broad and wide. Surely there is room for your men to hunt game and till the soil, and our men to hunt game and till the soil, without our paths coming together into a warpath. I have spoken!"

"Our Indian brother's words sound pleasant in our ears," answered Standish, who as leader of the soldiers acted as spokesman. "The land would be barren indeed and the sun always shine through clouds, if our Indian brother's face were turned against us."

These and many other flowery speeches passed between the men sitting around the council fire; for an Indian dearly loves speech-making and high-sounding talk. Long into the day the pow-wow lasted, and at its close an important treaty had been drawn up. Each side agreed to keep peace with the other, and to come to their aid in case of war with some third party. The Indians were no less pleased than the white men at this treaty, as it gave them the protection of the palefaces' guns, in case the Narragansetts or other tribes became troublesome.

In the years to come, the Pilgrims were to find their treaty of inestimable service. For more than half a century it was faithfully kept on both sides. Without it, the little colony might easily have been blotted out—just as many another— and the settlement of Massachusetts deferred for many years.

A few days after Massasoit's visit, Squanto was sent to him with the word that Captain Standish would return the call. This Standish did, accompanied by one man, Isaac Alderson, and Squanto. Acting upon a hint from the latter, Standish purposely refrained from bringing other men with him, as the Indians' supplies were low at the beginning of spring.

The Wampanoags received them with every evidence of friendship, and sat them down to a stew; what its ingredients were they refrained from asking. Besides this, the Indians could give them only a few groundnuts and a small quantity of tobacco.

With the coming of buds and blossoms and the first robins from the south, the weary pioneers began to take heart. It had required all their piety and fortitude to keep going through the long winter. No other ship could reach their ice-bound harbor, their supplies were fast dwindling, and death had laid its hand on one after another. Even their first governor, John Carver, and Mistress Rose Standish, the wife of the doughty captain, had been taken. Now with the first days of spring the sick ones began to regain health.

Squanto proved himself invaluable. He showed them how to set snares for game, and thus conserve their powder and shot—also avoid frightening off other wild creatures. The Indian hunts silently. He also showed them how to spear fish, which began to appear in large numbers in the sea. The waters of the Cape fairly teemed with cod—whence it had got its name, years before the Pilgrims came.

Another "stunt" that Squanto showed them was most useful. He had told them about the maize or Indian corn, which was the chief grain of the natives. This was to be planted, he said, in separate hills, with three or four kernels to the hill. They cleared some land for this purpose, and when the time came to plant they were surprised to see Squanto coming up the hill with a string of small fish.

"Do it this way," he instructed. He dug a shallow hole, placed a fish therein, and then on top sowed his corn. "The dead fish make fine corn," he said. And so it proved. He had given the first lesson in soil fertilization in America!

Other things were planted besides corn that year: barley, a little wheat, pumpkins, squash, beans, and a few other vegetables—some being entirely new to the settlers. But when Squanto said, "Try him—he's good," they went ahead without further question.

With the northward flight of the ducks, geese, turkeys, and other wild fowl, the larders of the Indians, as well as of their white neighbors, became well stocked. Then feasts could be arranged at one camp or another at short notice, and Massasoit sent word with much pride to his allies to come and share his plenty. He, however, was not the only chief who took notice of them.

One day a strange Indian strode boldly into the village and demanded audience with the white chief. He was ushered into the presence of Governor Bradford and Captain Standish. Without a word he laid before them a sheaf of arrows bound up in the skin of a rattlesnake. Then he stood proudly and glared at them, awaiting an answer.

"What is the meaning of this?" asked the governor of Squanto, although he suspected its purport.

"He comes from Canonicus, the sachem of the Narragansetts," answered Squanto. "He is an enemy of the paleface and means to drive him out of this country."

"If he wants war he shall have it," replied the governor.

Standish, on his part, unwrapped the arrows and took the skin. Holding it up before the savage he poured it full of powder and ball.

"Take it back to Canonicus!" he said.

The messenger accepted it gingerly; he was afraid of it and he showed it, but he did not dare refuse. He marched sullenly out of camp and for the next few days the colonists redoubled their vigilance. Then one day Squanto, who had

been doing a little scouting on his own account,
came back into the village laughing silently.

"The Narragansetts think your snakeskin
heap bad medicine," he reported. "When
Canonicus get it back from his scout, he not
touch it. He not let it stay in his village—afraid
something might happen. The scout he not touch
it again—he afraid. They hold council and draw
straws. Another brave gets the short straw, and
has to take it out of camp. He go to another
village, and they won't have it either. It goes
to three, four camps, and all say, 'Bad medicine!'
I think we get it back again and Indian not
fight."

Sure enough, within a few days an Indian appeared carrying the snakeskin gingerly. When
he came to the gate of the stockade, he threw
it down on the ground and fled precipitately.
That was the last of the threat of warfare for
some time.

Through the long days of summer the Pilgrims
toiled. There was a multitude of things to do.
The fields and gardens were tended, and new
houses built and old ones repaired. The stockade
was strengthened and guard constantly kept
against hostile Indians. Every one worked—
men, women, and children,—but the outdoor life
and abundance of fresh food made them rugged
and healthy. Squanto continued useful, so much

so that on one occasion when another tribe had seized him and held him as hostage—even going so far as to say that he was dead—Captain Standish marched against the offenders and threatened to exterminate them unless Squanto were delivered up to him at once. He was given up safe and sound.

At another time they took a small ship and coasted along the shore trading with the Indians and getting further supplies of foods and fruits, in exchange for beads and trinkets. They took this means, also, to explore the country. Squanto went with them on all these expeditions, his presence alone sufficing to allay many suspicions, while his knowledge of dialects made trading and conversing much easier.

In the fall a great contrast was afforded to the want of the preceding winter. Their harvests were gathered in. True to the scout's prediction, their corn had grown wonderfully. Other crops were good. Golden pumpkins shone in the sun. The busy housewives had cooked fruits and berries for winter use. The woods teemed with rabbits, squirrels, deer, bear, and other game—some good for food, others useful only for their pelts. The Indians showed them how to cure these skins, to make warm blankets and clothes. It was a time of plenty when Nature dealt out her treasures with a lavish hand.

"Let us have a great feast," said Massasoit; for with the Indian the time of plenty is the time to enjoy life. Too often he lives between feast and famine.

"Yes, let us feast," agreed Bradford, Standish, and the rest. But as they talked it over they decided to make it a feast of thanksgiving. The Pilgrims were deeply religious people. They held services daily. They felt that they had been in the shelter of God's hand, here in the wilderness. He had protected them and led them through. Now it was but fitting that they show their native allies their gratitude to Him.

Squanto was sent far and wide bearing the invitation to the feast, and the Indians gladly accepted. Massasoit came with ninety of his braves. What a barbecue it was! Wild turkeys, brought in by the Indians themselves, were roasted on spits. Pheasants, quail, ducks, geese, rabbits, all gave forth a savory odor. Over a trench filled with coals were two whole deer. Back in the kitchens the flushed wives turned out pumpkin pies, the first the Indians had ever seen, and an instant favorite; also fragrant cookies, doughnuts, and cakes. The children ran back and forth carrying platters of food, or replenishing the fires. It was a busy and happy time. The Indians and their white friends sat around in little circles, eating, talking, and laughing. By this time both sides knew many words of the other's tongue. They were comrades. For three days the feasting lasted, and it must have been a weary bunch of cooks when it was through.

Between-whiles there were games—running, jumping, wrestling, and other contests; target practice, where the Indians showed their marvelous skill with the bow and arrow, and the white men acquitted themselves creditably with their muskets. The children played games with their Indian playmates. It was a gorgeous feast there on the grassy slope looking out on Plymouth harbor.

Each day at morning and evening Governor Bradford caused a bugle to be blown and the whole company, settlers and Indians, stood at attention while he asked their minister to return thanks to the Heavenly Father for all his benefits. And the minister prayed long and fervently to the Father of all peoples—the Indian, the Englishman, and every other the world around. When he had ended old Massasoit would grunt, "It is well!"

With this pleasant picture we should like to close the story of the first months of the Pilgrim Fathers in this land; but we can seem to hear some voice asking, "What became of Squanto, afterwards?"

Squanto did not live to see the success of this first Massachusetts colony, which he had aided so well when it most needed aid. On one of the trading expeditions down the coast he fell ill of a fever. They brought him ashore and did everything possible to allay it, but without avail. Finding himself slipping beyond the reach of human help, he turned to his white friends and, pointing to a few chosen trinkets, he said, in a weak voice, "These are for you, my brothers."

Then turning to Governor Bradford, who was one of the party, and whose heart was torn with grief at the loss of this valuable ally and loyal friend, he said with failing breath:

"Pray for me that I may go to the Englishman's God. I—have tried—to be—friends!"

CHAPTER FIVE

FOR many years Massasoit, chief of the Wampanoags, lived to preserve peace between his people and the English. He saw their first, precarious settlement at Plymouth grow into a sturdy, self-supporting colony. He saw other English towns springing up on the coast, or a few miles inland—Salem, Boston, and a dozen others. His scouts told him of still other settlements down in what is now Rhode Island, and as far west as Deerfield and Springfield. He heard many tales of the unrest of the natives, as the white men crowded them more and more to the west. His heart was torn with conflicting emotions when the Pequot War broke out, and the Indians felt for the first time the terrible power of the invaders.

All this and much more had the friendly sachem heard and seen of the might and prowess of his paleface neighbors, but he counselled peace. He had given his word in treaty and it must not be broken. For fifty years or more the calumet was smoked between him and the leaders who succeeded Standish and Bradford.

At the many powwows which were held by the Wampanoags and the Pilgrims two interested young spectators were often present. They were the two sons of Massasoit, whom the white men had christened Alexander and Philip. But Philip, the younger, liked his Indian name best —Metacomet. As a boy, although educated in many of the paleface ways, he resented their assumption of superiority and clung to his tribe. He listened eagerly to the tales of the old men about what the country was like before the English came, and there were no towns to interfere with the hunting grounds, and the Indians might go and come at will.

To his mother, his chief confidant, he poured out his heart.

"Why is it," he asked her, "that we can go on the trail only at the white man's behest? Did not this land belong to us long before it belonged to him?"

"Yes, my son," she would answer; "but when you are a little older you will learn that might is stronger than right."

"Then I must make myself strong—stronger than the paleface."

"You must be strong in your body and strong up here too," she replied, tapping him on the forehead. "Learn the speech and the ways of the white man, but forget not the ways of your fathers. Then you will have the wisdom of a two-headed eagle."

"But if the ways of the white man are better—?"

"No man knows all the trails of the forest. Some of our young men have forgotten what their fathers and mothers taught them. They ape the white men. They shoot with guns and forget how to throw the tomahawk or speed the arrow. So they tell all the world, with their thunder weapons, every time they strike down an animal on the hunt. And their enemy miles away knows when they are on the warpath. I would have you shoot an arrow straight and far. I would have you hurl a tomahawk not to miss. Then you will be two-handed as well as two-headed. You will be a great chief!"

This and much more did his mother tell him, and Metacomet listened eagerly. But no hint of his hostile feeling toward the English did he show while his father was alive. Although he sat at the council fire and looked on and kept his peace, this was not noticed as it did not behoove the young braves to talk when their elders were present.

The Narragansetts, near neighbors of the Wampanoags, had more than once shown their unrest as the English built their towns closer and closer to them. Hemmed in by the sea at the south, they faced a time when they must either fight or move away. In this tribe was a young chief who afterwards became sachem— Canonchet. He and Metacomet, whose tribes had long been enemies, now buried the hatchet in their common mistrust of the white men, and often met and talked in secret. But no whisper of what they said leaked out to the ears of the colonists.

"The English are still few and scattered," they agreed. "The time to strike is before they grow many and strong. We are brothers."

When Canonchet was made head chief of his tribe he boasted a thousand warriors. Metacomet—or Philip, as he was known to the English,—led seven hundred warriors. Besides these, there were other outlying tribes that could be counted upon, in case of war. Philip's older brother, Wamsutta, whom the English called Alexander, must have heard something of these whisperings, but as a matter of policy he kept his ears closed to them. As head chief of the Wampanoags after his father's death he came and went freely and professed the same friendship for the English that Massasoit had shown.

One day at Plymouth he was called before the governor and closely questioned. Vague rumors had made the colonists uneasy in their turn. The Narragansetts and the Wampanoags had been enemies for generations. Now if they formed an alliance it would be dangerous. When the English began to make inquiries of Alexander, he drew himself up to his full height of six feet and met their glances unwaveringly.

"Wamsutta stands in the house of his father's friends and his own friends," he answered. "Why should there be doubt and distrust between us?"

And so they were not able to get any confirmation of their doubts from this wily man. Whether or not he was a party to the plot will never be known, as on the way back home from Plymouth, where he had been closely questioned, he took sick and died. When the news of his brother's sudden death reached Philip he was convinced in his own mind that he had been poisoned. It was the final straw with him. Henceforth he was the bitter enemy of the English, yet he must bide his time to strike.

His brother's passing made him the supreme power in his tribe, and he found his people ready and eager to listen to him. Tall and of commanding presence, he had that force of personal magnetism which makes great leaders. He had heeded his mother's admonitions. He could speak eloquently in both tongues. He could handle the rifle as well as the bow. He knew the stratagem of the English and the cunning of the native. The colonists came to call him "King Philip" and he well deserved the title, as his scouts went from one tribe to another and summoned them to arms in his name. He was the first really great leader the Massachusetts Indians had had in a century. But all this the English were to learn later, at their cost. Now they were only concerned with cementing anew the treaty which had stood for so long.

Philip came to Plymouth to talk with them, but he came attended by a retinue of braves and not at all in a submissive mood. He asked no favors at the hands of the English. To the governor he said proudly:

"You, my brother, do not own this land—even the land where your own houses stand. You are but an agent of the King of England. I shall not treat with an agent. If your king wants to make a treaty with me, let him come over in person!"

Nevertheless, Philip outwardly kept the peace for thirteen years. He became head chief in 1662 and it was not until 1675 that hostilities actually began. But in those thirteen years he was by no means idle. He sent his messengers secretly far and wide, bearing the black wampum belt.

"When this sign comes again to you—strike!" he commanded.

Like many another Indian outbreak, this one began with a trifling happening. An Indian convert to Christianity who served under Philip at Mount Hope at last could not keep back the news which he had heard. He reported to the English that a terrible uprising was being planned. Soon afterward the informer was found dead by the roadside. Suspicion pointed to three of Philip's warriors, who were seized and tried by the English and put to death.

Near Mount Hope, where Philip lived, was the little settlement of Swanzey. One day soon after the execution of the three Indians an excited horseman came galloping into Boston, crying for help.

"The Indians! The Indians!" he shouted. "They are burning down our houses and murdering our people!"

A group of citizens quickly armed themselves and took horse for the relief of the village. Long before they reached it, their worst fears were confirmed. Columns of smoke ascended into the air, and as they came nearer the screams of women and children were heard mingled with the war-whoops of the Indians and the reports of guns. The speedy coming of the rescuing party caused the Indians to take to the woods, but only after several houses had been burned and their families killed. Others taking refuge in the blockhouse had saved the village from utter destruction.

The English lost no time. Philip was indeed on the warpath. He must be seized before the conflagration spread. Within four days a party of soldiery was recruited from Boston to join with another from Plymouth, and both marched straight for Mount Hope. They almost surprised Philip, so quick was their coming, and he was seated at his dinner when they galloped into the village. He had barely time to escape from the further side of his camp and take to the woods. He had already taken the precaution to remove most of his supplies to a secret cache. Now he took refuge with his friend Canonchet of the Narragansetts, and the war was on.

But Indian wars are unlike others. There is no massed attack at any given spot; no blaring of trumpets or waving of flags. The sun on those June days that followed shone down upon quiet valleys and peaceful forests, as before. Now, however, when the farmers went out in the morning to begin their plowing or hoeing, they cast uneasy glances toward the fringe of woods, and while one man worked, another stood at guard not far away, his gun in hand. And well it was for them that they took this precaution. Within a week came tidings of another sudden attack upon a remote village. Out from the forest descended a horde of whooping Indians, fearful in their war paint. The scattered houses were quickly surrounded and one after another burnt to the ground, and men, women, and children tomahawked. Then the attackers vanished as suddenly as they had come—only to be heard from in another direction, some days later.

A great fear fell upon all New England. No one had any means of knowing how widespread was the league against them. It was known that King Philip had sworn to drive out all the whites and reclaim the land for the Indians. Whether he had only a few tribes with him, or all, none knew. The outwardly peaceful tribe living near some settlement might perhaps rise up against it at any moment. Who could tell?

As for Philip, he was everywhere and nowhere. He was a will-o'-the-wisp striking here to-day, yonder to-morrow. While they hunted him in the eastern part of the colony, news came that he was in the west. As they sought him in the north, word came that he had descended upon Dartmouth, Middleborough, and Taunton, with fire and tomahawk, sparing none, young or old. In the west, Springfield, Deerfield, Hatfield, and Hadley felt his vengeance. At Brookfield there was one house so much larger and stronger than the rest that all in the village crowded into it, when the dread news was received that the In-

dians were coming. But as there were few loop-
holes, those within could not fire upon the invaders, who came fearlessly close up to the walls
and tried to set fire to the building with long
poles on which torches were fastened. They also
tied burning wisps of straw to arrows and shot
them on to the roof. The people sheltered in the
garret then cut holes in the roof and put out the
fires. The Indians next filled a barrel with burning stuff and rolled it against the house, by means
of long poles. This threatened to get the best
of the besieged when, at the last moment, help
came from heaven. A sudden downpour of rain
put out the blaze.

"See! God himself has come to our aid!" they
shouted joyfully, and resisted the next attacks
so vigorously that the Indians went away.

Another strange story was told concerning the
attack upon Hadley. A special day of penitence
and prayer had been ordered, and the people had
all gone to the church. While they were on their
knees the terrifying cry was heard, "The Indians! The Indians!" The men jumped to their
feet; they had carried their weapons with them
into church, and now they sought to form into a
company in the village square. Judging by the
war-whoops which filled the air, the town was entirely surrounded; there were hundreds of Indians, and the defenders numbered but two or

three score. At this critical moment an old man with flowing white beard, looking like one of the prophets of ancient times, was seen coming down the street. He strode straight up to the men at arms and said with a voice of authority: "Follow me!" They fell in line behind him without question, although none had ever seen him before, and out against the enemy he marched. Arrows and bullets whizzed on every side, but the old man paid no heed to them. His appearance and the resolute fight offered by the townspeople struck dismay into the Indians and they retreated. When the fight was over all looked about for the aged leader, but he had disappeared as suddenly as he had come, and none ever saw him again. In later years when the children were told many tales of King Philip's War, and they asked, "Who was he?" their mothers would reply: "We do not know. Some said he was a hermit, and others that he was an angel sent from heaven."

Other queer tales were told of this dread year. Some said that a comet shaped like an Indian bow had been seen. Others said that the clouds looked like horsemen carrying flaming arrows; and that in an eclipse of the moon, a shadow in the center looked like an Indian scalp. All such tales go to show the general terror of the time.

At Northfield things did not go so well with the settlers. The town had been besieged for several days when a company of soldiers was sent to their relief. On their way they fell into an ambush and thirty-six were slain. Their heads were placed on the tops of poles which were set up along the road as a warning to other would-be rescuers. The settlers finally fought their way out of the town, which was abandoned to the flames.

The people at Deerfield had heard all these things and were on their guard. A company of soldiers was stationed there, and the settlers were very anxious to harvest and bring into town the ripened grain in their fields, as it represented a year's work and their supplies for the coming winter. Captain Lathrop, commanding a company of ninety sharpshooters, went with the farmers to the fields. Their route led through a piece of swampy ground alongside a brook, and required them to string out in single file. At the farther end the open ground narrowed and led into a thicket. Just as the advance guard entered this thicket a wild commotion was heard —the dread war-cry followed by a hail of arrows and bullets, for the Indians were armed with both kinds of weapons. Captain Lathrop and some of his picked men fell at the first fire. Others tried to form and make a stand against the invisible enemy, but strung out across the meadow they made shining targets. It was not a battle, it was a massacre. Of the ninety soldiers and perhaps two-score farmers, only eight escaped with their lives. It was spoken of ever after as "that black and fatal day, the saddest that ever befell New England." The name of the stream was afterwards called "Bloody Brook."

At the height of his success, it was said that King Philip had at least a thousand men under him. No part of Massachusetts, Rhode Island, or Connecticut was safe from his attack; yet few if any of the beleaguered settlers ever saw him, to recognize him. As they could not find him to meet him in open battle, the English decided to carry the war into the Indians' own country. An expedition numbering nearly a thousand white men marched south through the heart of the Narragansett territory. It was now December and a deep snow made progress difficult, but it likewise hampered the movements of the Indians. The Narragansetts had gone into winter quarters in three or four good-sized villages, the largest of which was on a small island in the center of a morass. The Indians had further fortified this natural stronghold by means of a high palisade of trees and logs. It was twelve feet high and very thick. Its only means of approach was by means of a large fallen tree which led from the single entrance to the village across to dry land on the outside. There were two thousand braves ensconced in this fortress, as well as the wigwams containing their families. They were ready to fight to the death.

Although the attackers were outnumbered two to one, and were in the open, they did not hesitate. They bivouacked the night before the battle in an open field a few miles away, bedding down for the night on the snow, and not daring to seek the shelter of the trees. The next morning at sun-up and after a hasty breakfast they were on their way. The Indians had kept scouts posted, and soon one of them dashed into the village with the word, "The palefaces are coming!"

When the attacking party came in sight of the fort they were greeted by wild whoops and a few stray shots, but they marched ahead determinedly. It looked, however, like a desperate venture. The Indians had all the advantage. The tree which served as a bridge was too narrow to allow of more than one man at a time upon it. Six times the colonists tried to rush across it, but each time the brave men were shot down and fell into the swamp below. They soon saw that an open attack was impossible; they must try strategy. While they continued to make a brave show in front, a party of men were secretly sent

on a detour through the woods to come upon the
fort from the opposite side. Here they were
fortunate in finding firm enough footing to get
across to the island, and by mounting on each
other's shoulders they climbed over the palisade
and dropped down safely and unobserved in the
center of the wigwams.

Presently the braves who were defending the
fort at the front heard a wild scream from the
squaws and children behind them. Turning they
beheld fires raging at a dozen places in the flimsy
structures. The flames quickly spread and carried panic and fear with them. The Indians had
fought bravely at the front of the fort, but the
surprise attack on their homes threw them into
a confusion. The Narragansetts, braves and
squaws alike, wildly sought safety in flight, but
the very security of their stronghold was their
undoing. They were caught like rats in a trap.
Whenever one of them sought to climb over the
palisade, he was shot down. To go out by the
front gate and across the log was equally fatal.
Some fought with the courage of despair, and
finally sought shelter in the woods. But many
Indians lost their lives that day, in one of the
most sanguinary battles fought with them in
New England. Worse still, a large quantity of
winter stores was destroyed. The survivors wandered all that winter through the forest, eking

out a miserable existence. It was cruel upon the women and children, but it broke the power of the Narragansetts effectually and badly crippled Philip's campaign.

Philip himself had not taken part in this battle, but Canonchet, his friend, and the chief of the Narragansetts, tried vainly to rally his tribe. He sent out his young men urging all to stand firm. "We will fight to the last man before we will be slaves to the English," he said. It was not long, however, until Canonchet was captured and taken to Plymouth for trial. His bearing before the white tribunal was as haughty as had been that of Philip. He did not recognize the authority of his accusers, and complained bitterly of the wrongs suffered by the Indians at the white men's hands. "I am but protecting the homes of my people, their wives, their children, their old men," he said. "Would the English do less?" The court tried to bargain with him, and offered him his life as a condition of securing peace. He drew himself up proudly at this and looked coldly upon the judges, not even deigning to answer. When the sentence of death was pronounced upon him, he said:

"I like it well. I shall die before I speak anything unworthy of myself."

Thus perished Canonchet—not on the field of battle, as he had hoped, but on the scaffold of a common criminal. Yet it was a prouder fate than that which came to Philip. As the settlers became better organized, the various tribes lost heart and began to fall away from him. He went farther west and sought an alliance with the Mohawks, but without success. He returned to Massachusetts and carried on a desultory warfare lasting into the next summer, of 1676. In May of this year a decisive victory was gained over the Nipmucks, at Turner's Falls, and three hundred warriors were slain. The English had meanwhile destroyed so many Indian villages that their people were faced with starvation and were compelled to sue for peace. Philip found himself at last with a mere handful of followers, dodging from place to place to escape the clutches of the soldiers. He went back to his old home, Mount Hope, and tried to make a last stand among his own people, but his pursuers pressed him so closely that he was forced to flee into the wilderness again, while his wife and child fell into the hands of the enemy.

A company of Plymouth troops under Captain Church drove King Philip into the swampland for his last stand. The Captain's men closed grimly around the bit of low ground where Philip was said to be in hiding. At last they sighted him—the man whom all New England had hunted for so long. He had perhaps a score of warriors with him, and he was still facing the enemy and preparing to do battle. Then at the moment of attack a shot was heard from the thicket at the other side. The great chieftain sprang into the air and then fell face forward into the mud of the swamp. He was dead— pierced by the bullet of an Indian spy who was an ally of the soldiers.

With his fall ended King Philip's War which was to go into the song and story of New England for all time. It had been a year of dread and terror when hundreds of homes had been burned and as many lives lost by the colonists. On the other hand, the power of the larger tribes —the Wampanoags, Narragansetts, and their allies, had been utterly broken. New England was to have peace from Indian assaults for many years, and her farms and towns could once more lie peaceful in the sun.

As for the instigator of this war, his name was one of terror for many a long year. Children were scared by the tales told around the blazing hearthstones of King Philip and his men. They were pictured as devils roaming around in human guise. Many of the tales of their cruelties were true. The Indian on the warpath is a fierce and often merciless opponent. Philip was neither better nor worse than his race. But according to his lights he was a patriot, seeking to protect and keep his country for his own people. What true man of any race or color would do less?

CHAPTER SIX

THREE hundred years ago, the country which is now Northern New Jersey and Eastern Pennsylvania was roamed over by scattered tribes of Indians of the same speech and customs, who called themselves the Lenni-Lenapes, which meant in their tongue, "the real people." The land itself was still virgin wilderness in which the scattered villages or tepees seemed a natural part. No axe had been laid to the trees, no gunshot had disturbed the stillness of centuries. The silent arrow of the Indian took its toll of the teeming wild life, but the great flocks of geese, ducks, turkeys, pigeons, quail, pheasants, and lesser birds, seemed to increase rather than diminish; while the forests were thronged with fur-bearing animals from the busy beaver to the lordly bear, and the streams were stocked with fish.

In such a royal hunting ground life was easy for the Lenni-Lenapes, who lived off the fat of the land. They dressed in winter in priceless furs, and in summer the squaws cultivated only a few scanty crops. Why should they toil when such a rich land was theirs? That was why they styled themselves "the real people." Their only source of annoyance was a more warlike people who lived at the north, the Iroquois, and who from time to time made incursions into their territory. Much ease had made the Lenapes indolent, and when their scouts reported the presence of wandering bands of these troublesome fellows from the north, they prudently retreated, rather than dispute the enemy's progress. Their villages were but flimsy shelters and easily moved. The wigwam poles with their coverings of skins or bark were down in a jiffy, as though a magician's wand had been waved over them.

Over the scattered tribes of the Lenapes a head chief arose, who—unlike most Indian potentates —held their allegiance through peaceful rather than warlike qualities. He was called Tammany, or Tamanen, and in the later years many stories were told about his virtues. He was just in his judgments, kind, hospitable, and wise. He sought to build his people into a strong nation, and to teach them other arts besides the chase. He encouraged the growing of crops, the building of better dwellings, and handicrafts such as the weaving of belts of wampum and basketry. So great a man was he that, many years after, when the white men had taken possession of the country, Tammany was venerated as a saint and societies in New York and elsewhere were named in his honor.

Tammany was only a boy living quietly with his tribe when the first white men came. Great was the excitement in the village when the runners brought the news. A huge, winged canoe had come sailing up the broad river, without oars or paddles, and had stopped where the two rivers meet. Then strange men with pale faces had come ashore, clad in garments which seemed to be made of shiny metal. They carried no bows or spears, but only knives, some as long as a man's arm, and another long, shiny weapon over their shoulders, as long as a man's leg. Such was the tale which excited the village, and now let us see who these white men were, and what it was all about.

The natural beauty of the country and its wealth of game had come to the attention of the Dutch soon after Henry Hudson had first sailed into New York harbor (using its later name). Every one knows about this visit, but what most folks do not know is the fact that earlier in his voyage he had tried to find an inlet farther to the south. He had received a letter from his friend, Captain John Smith, telling of the large bay there, and Captain Hudson thought it might prove to be the entrance to the Northwest Passage to India which he was seeking. Hudson sailed his ship, the *Half Moon,* into this bay, only to be stopped by shoals, so turned back. A year later, Lord Delaware, an Englishman, also visited this noble bay and was likewise thwarted by the shoals. The bay and river leading into it were called "Delaware" in his honor, and even the Indians living along its shores, the Lenapes, came to be known as the Delawares.

Had Tammany and his people been able to look into the future and see that both their country and their very name—"the real people"— were to be taken from them, it would have been galling to them indeed.

The first white man really to penetrate up the bay and river was Captain Hendrickson, a Dutchman. He it was whose visit was so eloquently described by the scouts in the village of Tammany's father. Hendrickson's vessel was called the *Restless,* and is worthy of special notice as having been built in New York harbor —the first so constructed. It was only a little over forty feet long and of light draft, and for this reason had sailed across the shoals which had stopped the larger ships.

Tammany went with his father to see this strange sight, and the strangers seemed peaceable but wary. Soon, however, a brisk trade sprang up, and the mutual distrust vanished.

The voyagers wanted fresh food and the skins which the natives carelessly wore over their shoulders. They offered in exchange bright beads and other treasures which the Indians secretly felt were far more valuable than the things they offered. But if the white men wanted to be foolish, that was their affair.

As Tammany grew to manhood, he saw still others of the men from across the seas. He found that they spoke various languages—they called themselves Dutch, Swedish, and English —and he further saw that they were mutually distrustful of the others' presence here. The Dutch sent ships and built a fort on the Delaware River, across from the site of the later city of Philadelphia. This was in the year 1623, by the white man's calendar, and its construction was an object of both wonder and dread to the Indians. By this time they had learned about the white man's gun and its terrors, and they saw visions of being driven from the home of their fathers, and of the game being frightened from their forests. While the incomers were still few in number, the Lenapes were not disposed to fight; they preferred to trade with them. But the more warlike Minquas at the south were hostile.

The Dutch built another fort down near the entrance to the bay, which they called "Swanen-

dael," or "Swan Dale." It was attacked by the
natives because of a queer misunderstanding.
The Dutch wished to lay claim to the country
in the name of Holland, but had no flag. They
therefore took a flat piece of tin and painted
the Dutch coat-of-arms upon it, which was then
nailed upon a tree. An Indian came along one
day, not long after, and his eye was attracted by
this gaudy emblem. Metal of any sort was
strange to the natives. It would make a fine
cup or pipe for him, he thought. So he proceeded to tear it from the tree and hammer it
into the desired shape. An indignant soldier
witnessed the act, deemed it an insult to his country, and shot the Indian. The tribe took no outward notice of the deed at the time, but later
surprised the fort and killed all save one of its
thirty inmates.

Although the Dutch built other forts along the
river, the Swedes were more successful as settlers. They bought the land for their homes
and farms, and by the time Tammany had grown
to manhood and assumed the head-chiefship,
several prosperous little Swedish settlements
dotted the Delaware bay and river. They built
towns on the later sites of Wilmington and Chester. An active trade sprang up between them
and the Lenapes, who in turn found it worth
their while to keep on the good side of their new

neighbors. Soon in the Indian villages might be seen pots, pans, kettles, blankets, and other unaccustomed luxuries; while the bright-eyed girls were dressed in gaudy calicoes and shawls. On their part, the thrifty settlers sent back home in a single year thirty thousand skins, besides cargoes of tobacco.

This peaceful, prosperous time was rudely interrupted by an armed expedition from the Dutch, who had been watching the growth of the Swedish settlements with jealous eyes. The invaders were led by the doughty governor, Peter Stuyvesant, whose wooden leg did not curb his activities. He hauled down the Swedish flag and raised that of Holland—only in turn to give way, within a very few years, to the greater might of England.

Something of all this turmoil Tammany and his braves saw, without understanding. The flying of a flag with one emblem or another meant little to them, provided the newcomers were friendly and did not trespass too far upon their hunting grounds. Around many a council fire the chief sat and talked the situation over with his braves.

"The Great Spirit has given us this land to hunt upon," he told them; "but still there is room for all. Far to the west we can go to the Great Mountains (the Alleghenies) and still the game

is more than we can slay. As for the white men
along the river, they have taught us many things
we did not know before, and have brought us
vessels for our food and new garments to wear.
We can spare them the shorelands they need for
their dwellings and farms. The Great Spirit has
given me still another message, also, about the
coming of the paleface."

He paused, but no one spoke or asked him a
question. They waited respectfully for him to
continue.

"For many moons our people were oppressed
by the Iroquois. The old men who are here and
who are wiser than I can tell you about their
ravages. Since the white men have built their
forts along the river, the Iroquois come no more.
If we remain friends with the white men, we will
be secure from the Iroquois."

"Good!" came from more than one throat;
and "You have spoken well!"

Thus it was that the Delawares made no ob-
jection when they heard of the coming of still
another great chief from across the water. The
English spoke of him as Penn, and when the
Indians asked what that meant—for to them all
names have a literal meaning—they could only
point to the quill pens with which they wrote.
So the Indians called him "Onas," which means
"quill" or "feather."

What further puzzled them was that he was called a "Quaker." "What are Quakers?" they asked. "Do you mean that they go about shaking through fear?" "That is not their true name," was the reply; "they call themselves 'Friends.'" "Ah, that is better!" said the Indians.

It was an English captain by the name of Markham who first told them about William Penn—or "Onas." The captain had come from England bringing news that a new settlement was to be made, and the land thereabout was to be called "Pennsylvania," or Penn's Woodland. The English king, Charles, had given him a generous grant of land for his colony, but Penn determined also to buy his land from his Indian brothers, when he came over in person.

Captain Markham himself brought a shipload of Friends, in July of the year 1681, but there had been much disease on the voyage, and the new settlers landed near Chester, more dead than alive. The other white people, both Dutch and Swedish, were kind to them and nursed them back to health. The Lenapes were likewise friendly, bringing them fresh fruits, vegetables, and game.

Tammany and Markham smoked the pipe of peace together, and the captain talked freely to the chief about the new plans. A town was to

be built at the junction of the Delaware and
Schuylkill rivers. This would make an ideal site
for a trading post, as the Indians could come
down the Schuylkill from the interior to trade,
and there was deep water close to the steep banks
of the Delaware for the ships.

"But first," concluded Markham, "my master,
William Penn, wishes to be assured of the friendship of his Indian brother. He lifts his hand
against that of no man. The Quakers never
make war—not because they quake, but because
they believe the Great Spirit forbids it. William
Penn will make a treaty with you, and purchase
the lands which he needs from you, if you are so
agreed."

"It is well," answered Tammany.

When another summer had rolled around,
William Penn came as he had promised. The
Indians who stood at the shore to witness the arrival of his ship then saw a curious ceremony.
As the small boat bearing a handsome and dis-
tinguished man grated on the beach, he was
greeted by the colonists with every mark of courtesy and respect. One handed him a cup of
water, another the branch of a growing tree, and
a third a bit of earth with sod upon it. This was
to acknowledge his lordship over the land. Then
all shouted and waved their hats, and the Indians

without knowing exactly why danced about and uttered whoops.

They saw in the newcomer a man who would attract attention anywhere. He was well formed and athletic in build, with sturdy shoulders and well-set neck and head, around which clustered dark curling hair after the fashion of the time. He had dark eyes, regular features, and smiled pleasantly on all about him. He awakened one's confidence at once, and the colonists instinctively felt that now they had a leader and governor indeed.

Penn lost no time in setting to work upon the new city, his pet project. It was to be called Philadelphia, or "The City of Brotherly Love." It was not to grow in rambling, haphazard fashion around someone's farm or following some cowpath. The streets were to be laid out at right angles, like a checkerboard. Those running one way would be numbered, First, Second, Third, and so forth; while those crossing them would be named for the native trees, Spruce, Walnut, Chestnut, and the like. There would be parks and central squares, all provided for beforehand. There was even a council-hall set aside for the Indians. Penn had obtained the services of a skilled surveyor in England, and had himself spent many hours on shipboard, poring over his beloved plans.

Best of all, he wished to build durably. The houses must be well constructed of logs, or brick, or stone; and as the settlers went to work with a will, fired with his enthusiasm, the natives watched with amazement the building of a town such as they had never dreamed of, or the New World had never seen before. But while they built these stout homes, each facing a straight street and at a straight angle, the builders lived in any kind of hastily constructed shelter, for it was summertime. Some even dug caves in the side of the steep river bank and lived there. Within a year three hundred and fifty permanent homes were built, and the City of Brotherly Love was no mere idea on paper. Within a score of years it was the chief city in the New World.

However, in his stress of building, Penn had by no means overlooked his promise to the Indians. He sent word at earliest opportunity to Tammany and the other chiefs that he would hold a council for the purpose of making a treaty with them and buying their ground. The Indians assented, and the place chosen for the council was Shackamaxon, near what was later Germantown. Hundreds of Indians and white men attended, as well as women and children, who viewed the whole affair as a huge picnic. Tammany and the other chiefs met Penn under a wide-spreading elm, near the river—a tree which stood for a century thereafter and was much venerated as the "Treaty Elm."

Here the pipe of peace was passed from hand to hand, and then Penn stood up and began to speak. Much of what he said they could not understand without an interpreter, but they liked the appearance of this handsome man who looked them straight in the eye and talked to them with straight, honest words.

"We will never do wrong to you or to any of your friends," he said. "We will live in love as long as the sun gives light."

"It is well!" the chiefs answered.

Then Tammany, now an old man but also of fine and noble presence, began to speak, and his words likewise were heard with close attention. He told of the land of his fathers and how it had looked before the coming of the white man. He told of the desire of the Lenni-Lenapes to live at peace with all men, even as these newcomers from across the sea. "If we make treaty with you, and smoke the pipe of peace with you, you will be our brothers!" he ended.

Again the calumet was passed from one to another, and then at a signal from Penn, men came forward carrying stout chests. They contained the goods to pay for the Indians' land. When their lids were opened, the Indians gave a little gasp of pleasure, for here were great heaps of bright beads, mirrors, combs, rings, knives, scissors, bells, and other things such as they loved. Here were also pots and pans, shawls and kerchiefs for the womenfolks. The Indians were well satisfied with their bargain and readily deeded over all the land set aside for Philadelphia, although the goods would not buy a foot of the city's ground to-day. Yet in view of the many miles of open country, the Indians had reason to be content with the trade. They were still more pleased with the appearance and words of the new governor. They hailed him as "Onas, our friend and brother."

This ceremony concluded, the more important business of the day was reached—at least, in the opinion of most of the Indians. There was a great feast, and what Indian ever could resist good food and plenty of it. They themselves had brought supplies—venison, quail, roasted acorns, hominy, tobacco, vegetables and fruits. The English had provided an ox which now hung in a ditch to be barbecued whole, and which caused the Indians to sniff appreciatively. The women had brought pastries, sweetmeats, and wines. Altogether, it was about the finest picnic the New World had ever seen.

The Indians behaved like children in showing their delight. They capered about, gnawing a bone held in one hand, and showing some gewgaw in the other. After the feast, or perhaps in order to make room for more food, they began to hold contests in running and jumping. Then it was that Onas sprang another surprise upon them. Laying aside his handsome velvet coat, he joined in the sport, and to the astonishment of the Indians, he jumped farther and ran faster than they did. For he had been a noted athlete in college, and was still a young man.

"Onas is a good fellow!" they exclaimed with delight. "We are proud to have him for a friend."

As the Indians became better acquainted with the Quakers, their confidence increased. "Onas always keeps his word," they told the tribes far to the west. And more and more Indians came down the Schuylkill and through the forests to trade with the white men.

The treaty made by Penn and Tammany under the elm that day lasted for seventy years, long after both leaders had passed away, and was respected on both sides. Penn did not remain long in America. Business connected with his grant called him to England, where he remained for fifteen years. He returned to find his beloved Philadelphia a bustling and prosperous city. He himself had a fine country estate a few miles up the river, with a handsomely furnished house and coach and four; for Quaker though he was, he liked fine clothing and furniture. But although dignified and courtly in his bearing, he was simple and direct in his speech to high or low, and he always held the friendship and trust of his Indian allies.

Again after a few months he was recalled to England, where he faced a powerful political plot. His colony had succeeded so well that it had awakened the greed and jealousy of enemies. At last his finances became so involved that he was cast into the prison for debtors, and only rescued by other Quakers. His last days were spent quietly in England, but he never came back to his colony, or saw his Indian friends, although he wrote frequent letters.

Tammany, the good chief, had long since gone to his fathers when, in 1718, news came to America that William Penn was no more. Traders in the city carried the news back into the wilderness.

"Onas, the Truth-Teller, is dead," was reported at many a council fire. "That was a goodly day when he smoked the pipe of peace with us under the Treaty Elm, and showed himself fleet of foot as well as strong of speech. We will keep our word with his children, for the sake of Onas, the Truth-Teller."

CHAPTER SEVEN

HOW PONTIAC BESIEGED DETROIT

PONTIAC, chief of the Ottawas, was troubled. From his island home across from the thriving fort of Detroit he had watched the trend of events, and it did not seem good to him. The French, whom he had been taught since boyhood to regard as his brothers, had been defeated at the hands of the hated English, and he liked it not. Had his French brothers not baptized him in their chapel and given him the mass in the name of their white God? Had they not given him firearms and fire-water, and gone on the hunting path and the warpath with him? Had they not lived in lodges as did his braves, partaken of the potlatch, and even taken Indian wives? But the English lived in their own towns and looked down on the Indians, even the Ottawas who were lords of the soil.

Pontiac well remembered the first time that he had met and come to blows with these vainglorious English. They had come marching across from the East as if they owned the whole country, and had shown their contempt of the

Indians by announcing their progress by the blaring of bugles and the waving of flags. Their general was a pompous officer named Braddock, who had boasted that he would clear the land of the French and Indians alike. Toward Fort DuQuesne on the Ohio he had marched, in open formation, not even sending scouts before him. Pontiac's nose wrinkled with scorn every time he recalled the day. Braddock had marched straight into a trap that the veriest Indian boy would have known how to avoid. Pontiac himself had commanded the Ottawas and Chippewas who fought alongside of their French brothers on that famous day. Before their sudden attack the red-coated enemy had crumpled like corn before the storm. Many scalps were taken and still hung as trophies in their lodges.

Pontiac's eyes sparkled as he turned and gazed at them; they were the most highly prized of all his possessions, and his fingers itched for still more from the heads of these hated English. His scouts and messengers had brought him distressing tidings. The English, far from being defeated, were coming back stronger than ever. For a few months after the rout of Braddock's forces the English had not dared to make a determined stand, and their settlements on the western frontier had suffered. Pontiac and his men were among the wandering tribes which roamed the Alleghenies and along the Ohio, taking heavy toll of the palefaces who had dared to come so far. Homes were burned, crops were devastated, and gory scalps torn from the still living victims. It had been a glorious time, thought Pontiac, but all too short.

Back had come the English, some of them red-coated troops from across the sea, but others plain backwoodsmen led by experienced colonial officers such as Colonel Washington. They were foemen worthy of the Indian's steel, and Pontiac knew it. Nor did they march against Fort DuQuesne alone. Pontiac learned that every fort in the long chain extending clear up into Canada was invested. Soon came the news that the French had been forced to sue for peace and give over all their posts and possessions to the English. Little wonder, then, that the chief of the Ottawas was troubled.

"Montreal is taken by the white dogs with red coats, and Quebec," his scouts reported to him. "Niagara has fallen, and Presque Isle, and Du-Quesne. Soon we will see the white dogs in Detroit and Michilimackinac. They are already beginning to bring their squaws back into the Ohio country and to clear the land, and our choicest hunting grounds will be no more."

"What my young men say is true," said Pontiac to the other chiefs. "The French were our brothers. They left the hunting lands undisturbed. But these English chop down trees, make clearings, build towns, and spoil the land utterly. They will drive out the Indians."

By the white man's calendar it was the year 1760. Pontiac's scouts had told him truly. The struggle known as the French and Indian War had ended in victory for the English. Canada had passed into their possession, and now that great section known as the Northwest Territory and later to be divided into the states of Ohio, Indiana, Illinois, and Michigan, was again attracting the attention of the English and colonial settlers. Across the Alleghenies they came, some by covered wagons, others by flatboats down the Ohio. Their progress across to the Mississippi threatened to cut the Indian lands squarely in two, as several famous trails led from the north to the south.

It was a wonderful game country indeed, rolling land with many watercourses and lordly forests interspersed with great grassy plains. Thousands of buffalo roamed here. Bears, wolves, foxes, and smaller fur-bearers might be found by the thousands. The air was filled with birds, the streams were stocked with fish. The simple wants of the Indians had been abundantly supplied. Now the coming of the paleface threatened to end all this forever.

Pontiac besides being a brave warrior was a man of keen vision. He foresaw all these changes which must inevitably happen unless the Indians united to drive out the invaders. He was a man of tall and commanding presence and gifted with an eloquent tongue. Now he began to go from tribe to tribe, stirring them into action.

"The leaves of the trees come out green in spring and turn red and wither in the autumn," he would begin in the figured speech that the Indians love; "yet still you sit in your wigwams until they are torn down from over your heads. The green leaves of spring are the incoming palefaces; they appear all over the land. The withered leaves of autumn are the Indians. Are you blind? Are you deaf? Are you no longer keen of scent? Cannot you see the curling smoke from his lodges, and smell the odor of his fires? Can you not hear the blows of his axe as he cuts down the shelter of the squirrel and the eagle? Or the reports of his guns as he scares away all the rest of the wild game that the Great Spirit has given to his children?

"Are your hearts like squaws', that you should slink away at his coming? Soon all your lands will be taken away from you, and you will have no food for the winter-time. This country is not large enough for both races. You must go on the warpath if you would hold what the Great Spirit

has given you. Why, then, wait until the paleface has become entrenched? Strike while he is
feeble and scattered!"

Pontiac did not speak as a suppliant. As he
continued his harangue he drew himself up to his
full height and his eyes flashed fire. He stamped
back and forth before his hearers and waved his
arms in sweeping gestures. He spoke with the
voice of authority, as a prophet and as a king.

"The Great Spirit says strike!" he hurled at
them; or, "I, Pontiac, will lead you to victory."

The Ottawa chief knew Indian nature thoroughly. This was the sort of thing that appealed
to them. Here was a leader indeed, they reasoned. One by one the tribes fell in line behind
him, from the Great Lakes at the north to the
Ohio at the south. Soon Pontiac was hailed as
king by thousands of braves—the Ottawas, Chippewas, Delawares, Mingoes, Wyandots, Shawnees, Miamis, Pottawotamies, and many others.
To those that he did not visit in person he sent
envoys—two braves, one bearing a black belt of
wampum, the other a red tomahawk, emblems of
war.

Pontiac had also learned other ways of the
white man. He kept tally of his men and resources. He issued his own money, a bit of birch
bark stamped with an otter, his totem, upon it.
His wampum was accepted over hundreds of

miles. While he could not read or write, he kept
two secretaries, one of whom scrawled out pictured messages to be sent to distant tribes, while
the other transcribed for him the replies that
were received. But so secretly did he work, that
neither secretary knew what the other was doing.
He was, in a word, wary, resourceful, and able
—one of the greatest leaders the Indians ever
had.

In this year 1760 he was informed that a detachment of English soldiers were on their way
from Canada to take possession of the fort at
Detroit. They were under the command of
Major Robert Rogers and were marching along
the southern shore of Lake Erie. Pontiac decided to intercept them and learn the plans of
the invaders at first hand. He came up with
them near where the city of Cleveland now
stands (although it was then open country) and
the meeting has been graphically described by
Major Rogers himself, in a diary of his expedition:

"As I approached Detroit at the head of a
military force I was met by an embassy from one
who came to let me know that Pontiac was at
a small distance, coming peaceable; and that he
desired me to halt until he could see me with his
own eyes. His ambassador had also orders to
inform me that he was Pontiac, the king and

lord of the country I was in. When we afterward met, he demanded my business into his country, and how I dared to enter it without his leave. I informed him that it was not with any design against the Indians that I came, but to remove the French out of the country, who had prevented a friendly intercourse between the English and the Indians. He thereupon told me that he stood in the path I travelled in till morning; and he gave me a string of wampum, as much as to say, 'You need not march farther without my leave.'

"When he departed for the night, he inquired if I wanted anything that his country afforded; and if I did, he would send his warriors to fetch it. I assured him that any provisions they brought should be paid for; and the next day we were supplied with parched corn and other necessaries.

"At our second meeting we smoked the calumet together; and he assured me that he had made peace with me and my detachment and that I might pass through his country unmolested, and relieve the French garrison—that he would protect me and my party. And as an earnest of his friendship, he sent one hundred warriors to protect and assist us in driving a large herd of cattle we had brought from Pittsburgh for the use of the army. He sent also to several Indian towns to inform them that I had his consent to enter the country. He attended me constantly till I arrived at Detroit, and was the means of preserving the detachment from the fury of the Indians, who had assembled at the mouth of the strait to cut us off."

The reason for Pontiac's pretended friendship was seen in the light of later events. His plans were not then ripe. He wished to lull the English into a state of security and then strike at a single blow every fort, hamlet, and farm. Thus and thus only, he reasoned, might the land be wiped clean of the invaders. So he welcomed the English into Detroit with an outwardly smiling face. His warriors stood gravely by and watched the lilies of France come fluttering down from the fort, and the Union Jack hoisted in its stead. He assured its new masters that the Indians were their brothers and would dwell in peace with them, even as they had done with the French.

For weeks and months this outward peace lasted, and meanwhile his emissaries continued to travel north, south, east, and west. The burden of their message was: "Wait—hold your hands. Make friends with the paleface—keep your counsel—and when the signal comes—strike!" So well were his injunctions heeded that no inkling of the widespread plot came to the soldiers in the forts or the settlers on the

plains. All over the land busy little farms began to appear, and roads to make their tortuous
way around bogs, through forests, and across
streams. To the lonely settler's wife the occasional passing Indian was no longer an object of
dread, beyond his petty thieveries. He was welcomed to the simple table whenever he chanced
to drop in, and would often appear at mealtime
bringing as his own contribution a fat squirrel
or brace of quail. In the forts likewise the
natives came and went freely. The French and
Indian War seemed indeed over, and all were
rejoicing in the piping times of peace.

Thus went the years 1761 and 1762, and the
first days of spring, 1763, drew on. It was the
most beautiful time of all in the Northwest Territory. The full foliage of the year burst forth,
and the fertile soil promised to yield a hundred-
fold to the plow and hoe of the busy settler.
With the month of May in hundreds of chosen
spots might have been seen the promise of the
later prosperous land. But back in the forests,
safely hidden from the white man's prying eyes,
was a vastly different picture. Again the black
wampum and red tomahawk had come from Pontiac, and with them the dread word, "Strike!"
Around the leaping flames of many a council fire
danced men hideously painted, who brandished
weapons and from time to time buried their

tomahawks deep into a stump of wood representing the enemy—which stood in the center. It was the war dance.

And—just as the cunning Pontiac had planned—the blow fell in a hundred spots without warning. The settlers saw the same men who had sat at meat with them now turned into fiends. With fire and tomahawk, arrow and bullet, the Indians sought to carry out their leader's instructions to the letter. None was spared, man, woman, or child. At least two hundred were slain on the day that ushered in this direful war, and for weeks thereafter the white men were hunted far and wide like animals. Ten forts were captured, some by stealth and some by assault, and many a sturdy little blockhouse witnessed a daring defense or hideous massacre. Only three principal forts stood out—DuQuesne, now called Fort Pitt, at the south; and Detroit and Niagara at the north.

On account of the importance of Detroit, Pontiac decided to attack it in person. His first moves, however, were by stealth, for he would not choose to attack openly what could be gained by cunning. He had managed to keep on such good terms with the garrison, that he might have surprised it but for one or two incidents which put the commander, Major Gladwin, on his guard.

A few days before the time agreed upon for the attack, a settler's wife had gone into an Ottawa camp to buy some venison. While there she happened to catch sight of some braves who were busily engaged filing off the barrels of their guns to make them shorter. Why should they do this—she reasoned—unless it was to make the weapons the more easily concealed under the Indians' blankets? But why should they do this in peace times? She related the suspicious actions to her husband, who went to the commander with the story.

The Major was not inclined to attach much importance to the incident, but fortunately received another warning. An Indian girl whom he had befriended came to him with a pair of beaded moccasins which he had commissioned her to make for him. She felt a great secret love for this soldier, and now as she handed over the moccasins, the tears began to trickle down her cheeks. The officer urged her to disclose the cause of her distress, and finally she broke down and told him about the plot. Pontiac and his men were to come the next day into the fort, ostensibly as friends, and would then kill every one in it. Major Gladwin soothed her fears and promised not to reveal her as the informer— then lost no time in making his own plans.

On the following morning, as she had predicted, out from the forest trail stalked Pontiac followed by a company of his warriors. Each wore a long blanket which he kept tightly wrapped about him, but as they were frequently dressed this way on errands of state, the garb would have attracted no attention. The haughty Pontiac paused when he saw that the gates, usually open, were closed. He demanded an audience with the commander.

"You may enter with twenty of your men," was the answer, as the gates were swung open.

Pontiac's keen eye darting from side to side, as he strode in, caught a sight which was not agreeable to him. Instead of seeing the soldiers sitting idly by as was their custom, now he saw that they stood stiffly at attention, and each man was armed. Further he saw certain well-known woodsmen, noted for their marksmanship, up on the walls with their trusty rifles in their hands. The shrewd chieftain knew in a flash that his plot was discovered, but he gave not the slightest sign of surprise.

"Why does my father keep so many of his young men standing thus with guns in their hands?" he asked Major Gladwin, as soon as they had exchanged greetings.

"To keep our young men from becoming idle —so that they shall not forget how to fight!" was the instant response, as the commander looked him sternly in the eye.

"My father need not fight when so many of his Indian brothers are ready to fight for him," insisted the wily chief. And he continued with a fine speech professing his undying regard for the English. It was, in fact, the speech he had planned to deliver anyhow. At its close he was to raise a belt of wampum high in the air, and this was to be the signal for his men to strike. He brought his talk to its conclusion, but just as he made a motion as though to lift his arms, the Major, narrowly watching him, drew his own sword and brandished it in the air. Immediately the long roll of a drum was heard, and the shrill blast of a bugle. The men at arms stood as if ready to fire.

With a quick movement, Gladwin stepped forward and tore the blanket from Pontiac's body. His guard did the same with the other Indians, and each man stood revealed clutching his sawed-off weapon.

"A fine friend you are to the white man!" the commander said, ironically. "Go, with your empty words and evil hearts! Go, before my young men fall upon you and slay you! I cannot harm you within the walls of this treaty chamber, although you yourself would not have respected it."

Pontiac glared at him, for once at a loss for words. Turning he stalked out of the fort with his braves, their scowling looks betraying the fierce rage and chagrin which burned in their hearts.

The next day Pontiac sent a messenger with honeyed words. Pontiac was sorry, he said, that there had been a misunderstanding. He would come again with his squaws and children, and they would feast together and smoke the pipe of peace. But Gladwin would not temporize. "Let Pontiac keep his distance," he warned the messenger. "The weather around Detroit is very bad; his women and children might take sick."

Seeing that he could not win by cunning, Pontiac threw aside his mask and became an open enemy. He laid siege to Detroit—a siege which was to last for many weeks. A thousand warriors lay in wait in the forests which came up within range of the stockade. They came and went, fresh men relieving others from time to time. Over the waters of the strait canoes came by the score bringing more warriors and supplies from the Canada side. Their plan was to starve the garrison out, and it looked as if they would succeed. The only source of relief for the beleagured fort was by water. White scouts had gotten through to Quebec urging succor, and expeditions were soon manned.

They had underestimated the power and stubbornness of Pontiac, however. When the first relief force came in sight of the fort, the garrison cheered and danced. They deemed their troubles were at an end. It was a large fleet of canoes carrying two hundred and sixty men, with food and munitions. Its commander was Captain Dalyell, who, not content with merely relieving the fort, was eager to teach these Indians a lesson. At the head of his men he dashed into the forest, intending to end the siege once for all by a bold attack.

The Ottawas and their allies met his attack with a spirited fire and then apparently retreated. Cheering, his men followed them. The Indians gave ground slowly and all that day the desultory battle kept up. Toward nightfall they had reached a small stream known as Parent's Creek, and on its far side the Indians had formed a strong barricade. Here in the gathering dusk they poured in such a murderous shot upon the tired soldiers that they in turn retreated—but not until over half of their number were slain. The waters of the little stream ran red with blood, and the fight was called ever after, the Battle of Bloody Run.

The effect of this victory for the Indians was to make them more determined than ever to take Detroit. They sent down blazing canoes and rafts in attempts to fire the walls. None dared to show his head above the stockade at any time. When other relief boats arrived from the East, Pontiac tried to set fire to them by allowing other blazing rafts to float up against them. Luckily for the fort's defenders, some of these boats got through, and so the garrison held out.

For five weary months the siege lasted—a thing almost unprecedented in Indian warfare, as the Indian prefers to win by surprise attack rather than lay a long siege. But this one was under the command of a super-chieftain, and the whole success of his war hinged upon the taking of Detroit. Little by little, however, his allies fell away from him. They met with reverses to the south, as more and more frontiersmen came up from Kentucky and across the mountains to the rescue of the settlers. The tide slowly turned, and by the end of the following year (1764) the confederation was broken and the Indians were in full retreat.

The little fort called Michilimackinac at the straits leading from Lake Huron west—later shortened to Mackinac—had a different story to tell. It was the first post founded in this section by the French. There was an important trading center, a mission, and a small garrison housed within the stockade. Here the Indians had dwelt at peace with white men ever since Father Marquette had established his mission, nearly a hundred years before. The good priests had baptized the children, ministered to the sick, and buried the dead. Many of the Chippewas who lived thereabout had become members of the church, at least outwardly.

When the French in this fort surrendered to the English, it caused not a ripple in the quiet of the post. It was so far to the north that its change of owners did not disturb the humdrum life of the little community. The Indians came and went as before, and the French peres were left in charge of their mission. So why should any Indian unrest at the south cause them uneasiness? However, rumors of Pontiac's plot did reach the English captain's ears and put him to some extent on his guard.

If the Chippewas had heard of the plot, they gave no sign of it. They went about among their old friends the settlers, trading and fraternizing with them. Some of the Indians had grown up in the shelter of the post. One bright June day they gathered on the parade ground in front of the stockade for a game of lacrosse, which was a favorite sport with them. It was played much the same as now. The contestants wielded long racquets and drove a ball from one side of the ground to the other. They were quite expert at it and their game was well worth watching.

As it grew more and more exciting, amid the whoops of the players and the wild cheers of the spectators, the garrison of soldiers, some twenty or more, with other white men, traders and settlers, came outside the stockade and ranged along the edge of the field looking on, and cheering some favorite player.

Back and forth went the ball before the swift blows of the racquets, the players surging madly about it. Suddenly an unusually vigorous blow sent it hurtling over the walls of the fort. A dozen players dashed through the gates after it. But once inside, the game suddenly took on a sterner aspect. The Indians dropped their racquets and seized guns and tomahawks which had been concealed underneath the blankets of squaws who had stationed themselves near the gate. In the twinkling of an eye they had changed from laughing players to shrieking warriors. Out upon the astounded soldiers they charged, killing all who stood in their path. The fort fell into their hands without a blow having been struck in its defense. Many in the settlement were slain in cold blood, and others carried off into captivity.

The treachery at this fort was duplicated in others. At one Indiana post the commander was lured into the woods by the story that an Indian was sick and needed his attention. While on this errand of mercy he was captured and his garrison slain. Only at Detroit and Niagara in the north, and Pitt at the south, as we have said, were the Indians unsuccessful. For many long weeks each was beleaguered. Fort Pitt was at last relieved by a small army of seasoned fighters, five hundred strong, who marched across the Alleghenies under the command of Colonel Bouquet. Their whole progress was a series of encounters with stray bands of Indians, for by this time the entire border was overrun with them. The seizure of one fort after another and the devastating of so many homes had made them blood-drunk. They believed themselves more than a match for the whites. Scalp-hunting had become a passion with them. Nor were they mean antagonists, as many of them were armed with rifles, which they shot with deadly accuracy. Driven off in front attacks, they hung upon the flank of the army like hornets and made its progress slow and dangerous indeed.

Colonel Bouquet was a veteran and soon got out of patience with this guerilla warfare. He determined to lure the Indians into open battle, even though he might be outnumbered—for he was by this time in the heart of the Indian country. He chose to make his stand at a place called Bushy Run, near Fort Pitt, and here he threw up a hasty barricade of trees and brush. On the next day, as he anticipated, the whole landscape seemed alive with Indians. They were dancing about and yelling, already gleeful at the prospect of victory and more scalps. Soon after sun-up they charged, only to be met with a sullen fire from the defenders. They broke and fled, only to charge again from another direction. Again they were beaten off, although at each attack some brave defenders fell. Time after time, through all that weary, bloody day, fresh attacks were made. While scores of the Indians fell at the unerring fire of the frontiersmen, it seemed that new men sprang up out of the ground to take their places.

Toward nightfall the Indians drew off, but the defenders, although ready to drop in their tracks, did not dare cease their vigil. The wounded were ministered to, and a strong guard was posted, which was relieved every hour as they took turns in snatching forty winks of sleep. At early dawn they prepared a hasty breakfast, and it was hardly eaten before the guard cried: "Here they come!"

The second day was a repetition of the first— savage, sudden onslaughts marked by brief breathing spaces. It was one of the most stubborn fights ever waged in this country. The Indians were determined to crush this invading host and to take every scalp. The white men knew that if they fell, Fort Pitt and Detroit would fall, and the clock would be turned back on the frontier for many years more. Each side fought with the courage of desperation.

At sundown on that second day the white army was wellnigh exhausted, but had managed to beat off the attackers on their last charges. What would the morning of the third day bring them? they asked themselves, as they posted another weary watch. But the sunrise of that day found them in undisputed possession of the field. The Indians had had enough of it, and were scattered and broken. It had been at fearful cost to the English. One-fourth of the whole force had been killed outright, and many others wounded.

This decisive battle marked the turning point in the war. Fresh troops were sent to the aid of Colonel Bouquet, who prosecuted his own campaign so relentlessly that, one by one, the tribes laid down their arms and sued for peace.

As for Pontiac, although repulsed at Detroit, he pinned his hopes to possible aid from the French at the south. He figured that if he could get into touch with the commander at Fort Chartres, in Illinois, or with others down the Mississippi, even as far away as New Orleans, he could enlist their aid to drive out the hated invaders. He went in person by canoe as far as Chartres, where the French commander told him that his war was useless; the French had made peace with the English, and he himself was really in charge of an English fort. Then he pointed out the Union Jack which now floated from his walls.

Pontiac grunted scornfully and turned away. Back he went up the Ohio, with many canoes in his train. At first glance one would have thought that he was leading his braves to a new attack. But not so. At the little post of Ouatenon, on the Wabash, he met some English commissioners who had been sent to conclude peace with him.

"You have fought your war under an evil star," they told him. "We will be your brothers, even as were the French. We will guard all your lands and respect your hunting grounds. Why have you followed this false trail and made war on your white brothers? It is useless. For every scalp taken, the Great Father across the seas can send a hundred fresh warriors. If you continue to fight, this country will know you no more."

Pontiac listened gravely and then called for the calumet—the pipe of peace. Taking a few puffs, he handed it to the English, who smoked in turn and then passed it back to his braves.

Thus ended Pontiac's War, and the treaty made at Ouatenon was later ratified in full council at Detroit, the fort he had striven so hard to take. At the end of the council, Pontiac rose to his full height, and taking his single eagle feather out of his scalplock, he cast it to the ground.

"Pontiac is no longer a warrior," he said; "Pontiac is now a hunter. He goes on lonely trails in the forest. He keeps peace with his white brother."

This peace the chieftain kept, but so long as he lived the English were still uneasy. Rumors kept coming to them, from time to time, telling of his secret plots. These rumors may have been the fabrication of his enemies, but knowing how successfully he had hidden his former plans, the English never relaxed their vigilance in his direction.

Some four years after the treaty of peace, or in the year 1769, they heard that he was again in Illinois striving to stir up the tribes there. He was not, however, the powerful chief of earlier days. He had become fond of liquor and spent many of his days in carousing. At Cahokia an Indian who held a grudge against him and was friendly to the English took advantage of his weakness and made him drunk. While in a helpless stupor he was stabbed in the back and slain by his betrayer.

When St. Ange, the French commander of Fort Chartres, heard of his death, he sent a squad of soldiers and conveyed his body into the fort, where it was buried with all the honors of war.

In breadth of vision, resourcefulness, and generalship, Pontiac ranks among the ablest of Indian leaders. He has left an indelible impress upon the history of the Northwest Territory.

CHAPTER EIGHT

W E are so accustomed, nowadays, to seeing maps of the United States with the various states set down just so, that it is hard for us to think of our country as anything different. Here lies Pennsylvania stretching out to the Alleghenies; and just beyond them lies Ohio. To the south of the Quaker state lies Virginia; and west of her, Kentucky. But if we go back two hundred years, these names do not mean much. Both Pennsylvania and Virginia, although still English colonies, were then reaching out greedily toward that land beyond the Ohio, vaguely called the "Northwest Territory,"—a land claimed also by the French, to say nothing of its original owners, the Indians. The English squabbled with the French over the land until the suspicious Indians remarked:

"If the French claim all to the north of the Ohio, and the English all to the south, pray where do the Indians' lands lie?"

Where indeed? The answer came in many a bloody encounter.

The end of the French and Indian War did not settle the question. Settlers from both Pennsylvania and Virginia pushed across the mountains and narrowly missed coming to blows over the ownership of the country. It was at the same time that Daniel Boone and his hardy woodsmen to the south were carving out the future Kentucky.

Meanwhile, the Indians were becoming more and more excited. They saw first one company of white men, and then another, come into the country and claim it. While the English and French might quarrel among themselves, the rights of the original inhabitants were given scant consideration. Often they were treated with the utmost brutality. The story of Logan is a case in point.

Logan was a noted Indian chief, of the Cayuga or Mingo tribes, who was born in Pennsylvania, about the year 1725. His Indian name was "Tah-gah-jute," which means "His eyelashes stick out." This referred to his keenness of vision and ability as a scout. Indian boys are named, on reaching manhood, for some distinguishing trait. As a young man he became the fast friend of James Logan, who served as secretary, and for a time governor of Pennsylvania, and because of this friendship he also took the name of Logan and was so known all his after life.

Becoming acquainted with the white men in boyhood and being kindly treated by them, Logan grew up of peaceful disposition. He supported himself and his family by hunting deer, bear, beaver, and other wild animals, bringing in many a canoe-load of pelts to the English trading camps. As more and more hunters came in and competition became keen, he pushed farther to the west, finally locating upon the upper waters of the Ohio. He was then about forty-five, a man of his word, respected by both races and wielding a wide influence. But the war-seeking braves never visited his lodge; they knew that he had been a lifelong friend of the English.

Just at this hair-trigger time when rival settlers from Pennsylvania and Virginia were looking for trouble, and prepared to meet it more than halfway, Governor Dunmore of Virginia sent an agent to the Indians, by the name of James Connolly. He attempted to enlist all the border Indians on his side, by specious promises, and did obtain some recruits, but only aroused the suspicion of other tribes. A rival agent, Captain Michael Cresap, becoming alarmed at reports of an Indian uprising, collected a force of armed men near what is now Wheeling, and

marched them north to subdue the natives. A
few Shawnees were killed, although some early
writers claim that they were not even on the
warpath.

A border desperado, Daniel Greathouse, then
became fired by the war lust and decided to organize a private war of his own. In those days
the borders were infested by many rough charac-
ters who paid little heed to the laws of God or
man. They plied the natives with cheap liquor
and defrauded them in trade. Whatever they
could get away with, they took. And so, with a
few choice spirits as unprincipled as himself,
Greathouse headed north on a rampage.

Encountering a party of Indians who thought
they were being summoned to a parley for trading, these ruffians fell upon them and slew them
in cold blood. In the band of victims were some
members of Logan's own family—his wife, sis-
ter, and children, according to some accounts.
Nearly a score fell in this abominable massacre.

The answer of Logan to this outrage was the
one given by Indians from time immemorial.
They lived up to the old Mosaic doctrine of "an
eye for an eye and a tooth for a tooth." Logan's
lifelong friendship with the white men was shattered, when other braves burst into his lodge with
the news, and the taunting cry of "*Now,* what
will be your reply?"

Lifting his two arms toward the sky in a gesture of vengeance, he seized his long hunting-knife and strode out on the warpath. With a picked body of Shawnees he fell upon the nearest settlements, slaying men, women, and children without mercy. He had become pitiless overnight. Soon the border was ringing with his name as an omen of fear, and the other tribes taking heart began to organize for real warfare.

As more and more ominous reports began to filter in to Lord Dunmore, he resolved to collect a strong force of fighting men and go out and crush the rebellion. It was in the troublous days just before the Revolution (1774), and Dunmore was having other troubles of his own at home. But the Ohio Company, as it was called, had too much at stake to allow the Indians to get the upper hand again. He assembled two divisions in the Shenandoah Valley, and took command of one himself, entrusting the other to General Andrew Lewis—a seasoned Indian fighter of powerful frame, who as a young man had seen service with Washington, at Great Meadows, in the French and Indian War.

Lewis started west in September, with two regiments numbering eleven hundred men. Their march was an arduous affair, as nowhere in the East are the mountains more rugged than here, and in those days there were no roads of any kind. Both ammunition and provisions had to be carried over on pack-horses. A narrow trail had to be cut through the pathless woods for them, and it was nearly a month before the army reached Point Pleasant, at the mouth of the Kanawahe River, on the Ohio. No word had been heard of Lord Dunmore and the other division, but alarming reports were brought in by the advance scouts of the presence of a large force of Indians—as large if not larger than their own troops—all in war-paint and chanting their war-songs.

It was a body of warriors which had been recruited by Cornstalk, an ally of Logan's. He was a powerful Shawnee chief who lorded it over the tribes scattered along the Scioto, in Ohio. At this time he was about fifty years old, and he was famed through all the Indian country round about for his prowess and courage. He was to prove, in this great battle with the settlers, that he was also a general of no mean ability. His own scouts had told him of the progress of Lewis's army, but it had marched in such compact formation and so cautiously that there had been no opportunity for ambush or surprise.

Cornstalk, therefore, elected to attack in the open, although he knew that the other force was equal to his own. By making a sudden onslaught he counted upon throwing the enemy into confusion. But the frontiersmen opposing him were quite as hardy and resourceful as his own warriors. After the first shock, each side grappled with the grimness of bulldogs, resolved to fight to the death. The Indians had prepared for this attack by choosing a wooded spot, in which they had erected a barricade, much as was done later by Little Turtle at the Battle of Fallen Timbers. Shielded by this rampart, the Indians poured a withering fire upon the advancing Virginians. Many of them fell at this fusillade, among them a brother of General Lewis. The general lighted his pipe at the beginning of hostilities and sat his horse watching coolly the attack of his first line. Seeing them wavering, he spurred his horse forward, then dismounted to lead up the reserve.

Still the Indians stood firm, and above the din of conflict a stentorian voice could be heard shouting, "Be strong! be strong!" It was Cornstalk running here, there, and everywhere among his men, unmindful of his own danger, urging them into the fray. And the Indians held. All that forenoon the fighting continued without definite result on either side. Then Lewis resorted to strategy. He sent a party off to one side to make a detour through Crooked Run, and thus fall upon the Indians from the rear. In an hour or so, a volley of muskets on the far side of the enemy proved that this had been accomplished.

At the report, he ordered his own men to charge. The surprised Indians turned in a panic. Again the voice of Cornstalk boomed out, "Be strong! be strong!" One fleeing brave he struck to the ground, his skull cloven in twain with a single powerful sweep of his axe. But the flight could not be stopped. The Indians were now in full retreat and did not stop until they had reached the Ohio. By sunset the field was cleared of the enemy.

But at what a cost! No less than twelve officers and seventy-five men were killed, and twice that many wounded, and they were the picked stock of the entire border. In many a home was mourning, following this bloody Battle of Point Pleasant, one of the most sanguinary in the whole history of that region. The plan of Cornstalk had undoubtedly been to defeat Lewis's force before he could unite with Dunmore; and then fall upon the latter. With the example of his success at Point Pleasant to inspire them, nearly every tribe north of the Ohio would have followed him.

Now, cowed by defeat they were ready to sign the peace treaty—all, that is, save one tribe, and that was the Mingo, headed by Logan himself. When invited to join the peace conference, he declined. His reply full of biting scorn has been preserved to us as one of the finest examples of

Indian eloquence. We can imagine the tall, impressive chief, standing with head thrown back defiantly, his blanket folded closely about his shoulders, his voice rolling in fierce denunciation at his wrongs. Here is his speech, according to the early historians:

I appeal to any white man to say, if ever he entered Logan's cabin hungry, and he gave him not meat; if ever he came cold and naked, and he clothed him not? During the course of the last long and bloody war, Logan remained idle in his cabin, an advocate for peace. Such was my love for the whites, that my countrymen pointed as they passed, and said, "Logan is the friend of the white men." I had even thought to have lived with you, but for the injuries of one man. Colonel Cresap, the last spring, in cold blood and unprovoked, murdered all the relations of Logan, not even sparing my women and children. There runs not a drop of my blood in the veins of any living creature. This called on me for revenge. I have sought it; I have killed many; I have fully glutted my vengeance. For my country, I rejoice at the beams of peace. But do not harbor a thought that mine is the joy of fear. Logan never felt fear. He will not turn on his heel to save his life. Who is there to mourn for Logan? Not one!

Although not a party to the treaty of peace, Logan abided by it and laid aside his weapons. Cornstalk did likewise, and his later fate does not make pretty reading. It proves very clearly

that treachery was often used by white men as a
weapon of war with the Indians. Cornstalk, having proved himself a general of high calibre, was
naturally feared by many of the settlers, who
expected him to incite another uprising. But
for three years, or until the year 1777, he kept
his word and remained at peace. Then the tribes
around him became troublesome, and tried to get
him into a new plot. Instead, he went to Point
Pleasant, where there was now a stockade, and
demanded a parley. He told the commander of
the threatened trouble, and that he feared he
might be drawn into it.

"Cornstalk will not strike in the dark; he fights
in the open!" he said, proudly.

Alarmed, the captain detained him and his son
as hostages, against another uprising. While
they were prisoners, a scout came, one day, to
report the killing of a settler a few miles away.
It was the act of some irresponsible band of
roving Indians, but the infuriated soldiers chose
to place the blame upon Cornstalk. Both he and
his son were put to death.

For this cold-blooded deed, which can find no
excuse, the Shawnees were fired to the highest
pitch of vengeance. They went again on the
warpath, and for seventeen years their name was
feared throughout the border. They fought with
Little Turtle in his disastrous defeat of St.

Clair,[1] and willingly served under any banner that meant the extinction of the hated white men. An Indian never forgets.

Meanwhile, what of Logan? He did not go again upon the warpath, so far as history records. He refused to be drawn into the powerful confederation organized by Little Turtle. Only one serious blot remains upon his later life story. He became addicted to drink. It was the common practice of the traders at the frontier posts to ply the natives with whiskey, and thus to get the better of them at the trade. Although Logan was aware of their purpose in handing out liquor so freely, he was not strong enough to resist it. The white man's fire-water did far more than the white man's firearms in his undoing. He presented a pathetic figure in later life, reeling about the trading posts. His end, in fact, came in a drunken brawl. One other story, however, is preserved to us, showing the better side of his nature.

Simon Kenton, the noted scout, had been captured by the Indians. Second only to Daniel Boone in fame, in the Middle West, he had known that veteran and had taken part with George Rogers Clark in the famous expedition of frontiersmen which had wrested Kaskaskia and other forts from the British, and had thus

[1] See the story of "Little Turtle."

ensured this entire section to America, and not England, at the close of the Revolution. The story of that march for hundreds of miles through the wilderness, and the surprise attack which followed, is one of the most romantic in our history. Simon Kenton's own story is not less so. He ran away from home before he was grown, crossed the Alleghenies to the west, alone and in constant danger of wild beasts and Indians, but survived to become one of the crack shots and most reliable scouts of the country. During the Revolutionary War, when many of the tribes adhered to the British, he went on various dangerous missions, and the stories of his exploits were told in many an Indian lodge as well as frontier camp.

One such adventure, among the many, will serve to show his courage and resourcefulness. He and another scout were paddling downstream in a canoe, when bullets began to rain upon them. Knowing that they would be hit, or their canoe punctured, as they made a shining target, they bent to their paddles and swiftly drove their canoe into an inlet on the opposite bank from the shots. Beaching it, they stole softly forward to see if this coast was clear, but in so doing Simon's foot slipped in some loose sand, and instantly a grunt of surprise told them that other Indians were near. Simon turned just in time to see the glint of a rifle barrel, as it was sighted in his direction, and instantly fell forward to escape the bullet which whizzed over his head. Meanwhile, the other scout had come to grips with another Indian.

Seeing Simon down on his knees, the Indian sprang forward with an exultant yell to finish him. He was a tall and magnificently formed warrior—half a head taller than Simon, who was himself of fine physique. Trusting to his superior strength, the Indian disdained to use any other weapon, but came to grips in a regular bear hug. Simon had just time to leap to his feet and meet the giant face to face. What made things worse was the presence of still another Indian, of whom Simon caught a startled glimpse just as he came into the clutches of the giant. The other Indian, who was of slighter build, had a rifle and was trying to get a pot-shot at the scout, but could not fire at him without risk of hitting his comrade. Simon's safety—if it could be called such—lay in this bear hug. But what a grip it was! Athlete though he was, he felt like a child and that the breath was being squeezed out of his body. Still he exerted all the pressure of his own brawny arms to hold the big fellow at bay.

Then the shorter Indian, circling round, came up behind him and tried to bury his tomahawk in his skull. Simon gave a convulsive kick with one of his legs and had the luck to land in the middle of the fellow's stomach, knocking him over into the river. The current was rapid at this point, and the last that Simon saw of him was his body being dashed about among some sharp rocks. The big fellow was so surprised at the fate of his comrade that he relaxed his grip a trifle. It was very little, but in that split second Simon's own hands sprang up and clutched him about the throat. It was now the Indian's turn to choke and strangle. With a throaty sound like a maddened animal, the giant caught the scout by the middle and literally threw him over his head. Simon went sprawling his full length on the sand, which fortunately broke the force of his fall, and what was his joy to clutch the rifle dropped by the Indian that he had kicked into the river. He rose and fired in one motion, without taking time to sight. The giant, in the act of rushing him, got the bullet through his heart.

After many such hair-breadth escapes, the scout was nevertheless captured at last. Great was the joy among the hostile tribes when the word went round that he was a prisoner. He was made to run the gauntlet—a long lane of his enemies in which even the women and children wielded some sort of weapon to strike the naked

victim as he dashed by. But the wily Simon
again outwitted them by breaking through the
line where it was weakest and making straight
for the council-house. By the Indian law, any
prisoner who reached this refuge was safe from
further attack for the day. His fate was to be
further considered.

At this critical juncture, who should come into
camp but Simon Girty, the notorious renegade
who had turned Indian and spy against his own
race. In all the annals of the Middle West there
is no name more hated than his, as he added to
his other crimes an almost unbelievable ferocity
against white prisoners. However, some years
before when Girty was still an accredited white
scout, Kenton had saved his life. Girty had not
forgotten this service, and when he recognized in
this bruised and bleeding victim his former comrade, a spark of his former manhood was re-
kindled in his breast and he made an impassioned
speech pleading for his friend's life. Many of
the braves were insistent upon burning the
prisoner at the stake. They recited the long list
of wrongs they had suffered at his hands. But
Girty taunted them daringly.

"My friend is not at fault for this," he declared. "You yourselves led a war-party against
the whites and were defeated; many of your men
were killed. But my brother is not to blame be-

cause you came within reach of his rifle, or because he can shoot straighter or quicker than you. Blame your own guns that do not shoot as swiftly or as surely as the white man's! Do not seek to revenge yourselves upon the only white man you have been able to capture. He has run your gauntlet; he is a man and my friend; I demand his life!"

It was, as we have said, a daring speech to make, but Girty knew the Indian character, and also he had been of great service to them. However, a torrent of protests greeted his appeal, and around the circle was seen the signal of death. Then Girty resorted to strategy.

"If you must kill my friend," he said, "why not make a fitting event of it? His name is known and feared in all the borders. Why not take him with you to the Great Council at Sandusky, and let your brothers there witness and add to his death agonies? You will also enlarge our tribe's renown by bringing in so famous a prisoner."

Grunts of approval greeted this suggestion, and it was finally voted upon favorably. Girty knew it was only a respite, and so informed his friend when he had later opportunity to whisper to him.

"You must die at the stake, up at Sandusky," he told him, "unless you can make a break for

it somewhere along the trail. I can't help you
any more, as they're all as mad as snappin' turtles, and they'll have a weather eye on me, too."

Kenton thanked him, and began to cast about
in his own keen mind as to ways and means of
escape. He knew that the tribes were all sullen
over their recent defeat, and would gloat over
his own sufferings as a partial revenge. "Mad
as snappin' turtles" just expressed it.

The march north from one village to the next
was a series of torments for poor Simon. He
was dragged along with his arms tied tightly to
his chest all day, so that they felt as if they would
drop off at sunset. At each village, the women
and children would dance about him, sticking
splinters into his flesh. For day after day they
marched him along rapidly, trying to break down
his stoicism and hear him beg for mercy. But
he only compressed his lips, resolved to march
until he dropped in his tracks, without a sound.

At the end of a long, gruelling day they came
to a good-sized village on the Scioto River. Here
when released he fell rather than sat down, and
began to munch greedily upon a bit of dried
bear's meat which they had given him. As he
gnawed it, more like a wild animal than a man,
a shadow fell across his path and he looked up.
He saw a tall, well-built chief of middle age,
but carrying himself so erectly that he looked

not much more than thirty. He was dressed in a manner to betoken a chief of high rank. A bright red blanket was thrown over an embroidered shirt of deerskin. His leggings and moccasins were also beautifully embroidered. A single eagle's feather stood in his scalplock.

The two men gazed a moment at each other, without speaking. In the mind of each at this moment was the thought: "Here is a man!" The chief was the first to break the silence. In perfect English and in a soft, well-modulated voice, he said:

"Well, young man, these warriors seem very mad at you."

"Yes, sir, they are," replied Simon, surprised at his address and the unexpected kindness of his tone. "I reckon as how it's all up with me."

"Don't be too down-hearted; the fire at the stake is not lighted yet, and the wood may be damp. You are to go to Sandusky to-morrow, I understand,—they speak of burning you there— but I am a powerful chief, and to-morrow I shall send two of my young men along to speak a good word for you."

Before Simon could thank him, the chief folded his blanket still closer about his broad shoulders and stalked away.

"Who is he?" asked Simon of his guard.

"Logan," answered the brave.

At the reply, Simon's spirits rose amazingly. He had often heard of Logan and knew that his word carried great weight in the councils. Lying down upon the ground he soon fell into the deep sleep of exhaustion. He was awakened at sunrise by a man touching him on the shoulder. Looking up he again saw Logan.

"Eat, my son," he said, pointing to food, "for you have another long journey to-day." He said not another word as to Simon's fate or his own plans, but walked out as abruptly as he had entered.

Thanks to his kindness, however, and the food, Simon's march was much more bearable that day. At nightfall they reached the big encampment on the Upper Sandusky, and there were greeted with loud shouts of joy, when the prisoner was discovered and his identity made known. Preparations were immediately begun for a big bonfire the next day, with Simon as its center—the women and boys industriously bringing in huge armloads of wood.

That night, in spite of his danger, Simon again slept soundly. He had been in tight places before, and knew that it behooved him to catch his rest when he could get it, and let the morrow's problems take care of themselves. At daybreak he was brought into the open space where the burning was to be held, and as a preliminary his face and body were marked with broad black streaks, giving him a hideous appearance. For two or three hours he stayed there tied to a stake, while the Indians big and little came by to peer into his face and taunt him.

Then another interruption occurred, in the person of a British officer, gay in his regimentals and epaulets, who came riding up. Dismounting from his horse and without so much as a glance at the condemned man, he began to address the braves in council. After a lengthy harangue—for all Indians like speech-making—he concluded with these words:

"I notice that you have already had a great deal of fatigue and trouble with this prisoner, without being revenged upon him. But he is only one white man, and your revenge would be slight. This man knows many things about our enemies that I am very eager to know—things that would be of advantage to you also, when next you go on the war-path. I wish to take him back with me to Detroit, and there question him. Then I can bring him back, and you can burn him."

"No, no!" shouted several voices in quick protest, "we want to burn him now. He stole some of our horses!"

"I will pay you for the horses," answered the officer. "And this man, with all the information pumped out of his head, will be much more valuable to us than burned to ashes to-day with all that information still in him. See, here is money for your horses."

He produced a roll of bills, and the Indians, looking first at the money and then at their victim, held a long powwow. At last, however, they yielded and Simon was unbound and turned over to the officer. The latter immediately gave orders that he was to be given some food—he had eaten nothing since the night before—and that his tattered clothing which had been torn from his back should be restored to him. Then he was given a horse and rode away with the officer and his guard, while the disappointed Indians scowled after them.

Once out of earshot and eyeshot, the officer rode alongside of Simon and smiled at him.

"That was a pretty close call for you," he said. "I am Captain Peter Druyer, of the Canadian forces of his Majesty, and at your service. I am connected with the Indian Agency, and am often called in to act as interpreter and go-between; so the Indians do not like to cross me. I heard about you through two of Logan's young men. Now I like to keep faith with my Indian allies, but this is one time that I am going to break my word with them. I shall not take you back to the Sandusky."

"You are sure white," began Simon, huskily; "how can I get square with you?"

"Don't thank me," answered Druyer; "thank Logan. He's one of the whitest Indians I've ever met."

"You're right there, pardner," agreed Kenton, heartily; "he's one of the very whitest!"

CHAPTER NINE

"THE Indian's lands are not for sale; they are his forever!"

The sachem who uttered this defiant speech drew himself up proudly and glared into the faces of the white men. The other Indians, squatting on the ground, folded their blankets the more closely around their shoulders and grunted their approval.

General Arthur St. Clair, a grizzled veteran of the Revolution, gazed into the eyes of the speaker with ill-concealed uneasiness. He had been sent by President Washington to placate the Miamis and their allies, but they refused to treat with the white man on any terms having to do with the further surrender of their beloved Wabash country.

The Indians felt that they were right in this attitude. They had watched the gradual encroachment upon their territory with increasing dismay, ever since the time of the first French traders and trappers. Their French brothers of the old days had not been so bad. They had

167

fraternized with them, hunted with them, and even married into their families. They had respected the Indians' desire that they leave the hunting lands untroubled by houses or clearings. But with the coming of the English things were different. The English saw in this land only a territory for the building of forts, towns, and farms. Before the ringing blows of their axes, the wild beasts were frightened away. Soon there would be no more furs or fresh meat. Thus argued the old men before the council fires.

The driving out of the English by the victorious Americans only hastened that dire day. The new power to the East, called the United States, now claimed full control of the Northwest Territory—as they called it—and was sending soldiers out to enforce its claims. These were the rich lands out of which were later carved the great states of Ohio, Indiana, Illinois, and Michigan. And already towns were beginning to appear, from Detroit and Cleveland, on the Lakes, to Marietta and Cincinnati on the Ohio at the south. As the chain of forts and towns crept westward, the Indians saw their hunting lands cut squarely in two, and they themselves hemmed more and more closely into the interior.

It was not in Indian nature to sit idly by and watch the paleface settlers accomplish this. Many were the attacks. small and large, made against the incomers. As their flatboats floated down the Ohio, or their wagons crawled across the prairie country, a shrilling warwhoop and a flight of arrows told the immigrants that they could only win a home in this wild land by fighting for it. The story of the settlement of Ohio and Indiana, consequently, is full of bloodshed.

General St. Clair was not the first American who had tried to treat with the Indians. The intrepid George Rogers Clark had held them in check by his very audacity, and when the name of "Long Knife" was mentioned in their councils it was only with respect. He was succeeded at Vincennes by General Josiah Harmar, who held a protracted treaty council with the Shawnees and other tribes along the Wabash. But despite his efforts they were growing more and more restless. He began to hear rumors of a powerful Indian confederation, under the leadership of a warrior called "Little Turtle." Who this leader was, let us trace back in their own tribal annals.

About the year 1752 there was born a boy into the tribe of the Miamis living on the banks of the Eel River, in Indiana (to give the country its later name). But as the boy grew up, he roamed at will through the unbroken wilderness, trapping beaver in the many small streams and bogs, trying his arrows upon the squirrels and chipmunks, or watching his mother and the other

squaws till their little patches of open ground
for their crops of corn and vegetables. It was
a pleasant land, on which the Indians roamed
and hunted, getting a living with little effort.
The only cloud in their sky, beyond an occasional
fight with some other tribe—which they took as
a matter of course—was the presence of the white
men in their land. At first scattered and few
in numbers, they were multiplying, and the boy
heard scraps of conversation from the talk of
the warriors in council which sounded ominous
indeed to him. These interlopers of white skin
were greedy and dangerous men, whom he in
turn must fight, one day, if his people were to
continue to live in the lands of their fathers.

Such was the early education of Michikinikwa,
who was later famed and feared as Little Turtle.
His father was a Miami chief, and his mother
a Mahican. By the law of the Indians he followed his mother's tribe; he was a Mahican and,
as such, not eligible to his father's rank. But
as he grew to young manhood his frame filled out
with splendid grace. He could outrun the other
young men, and endure more hardship. His eye
was keen as the eagle's, his hand unerring at the
bow. When he was given his first gun—the
weapon of the paleface—he carried it with him
night and day; he even slept with it; and within
a few days he knew its mechanism thoroughly

and could send its leaden messenger with the same unerring precision that he had sped his arrow.

Michikinikwa had an old head upon his young shoulders. He learned about the horses that were used by the white men for hauling their wagons and for riding. As soon as his voice was heard at the council fire, he began to urge that the wild ponies of the plains be caught and tamed for the Indian's use—which was done. Then he urged confederation with other tribes, to resist the white invaders. Striding back and forth before his listeners, he waved his powerful arms in telling gestures, as he pleaded with his people to unite.

"O, ye small handfuls of men!" he would say; "I see the Great Spirit scattering you before the blast like the sands of the shore!" Here he spread his fingers wide, as though allowing sand to trickle through them. Then bringing them together and clenching his fists he said: "Naught can escape the closed fist, although the single fingers are powerless. Each little tribe is no better than my little finger; but coming together to form the fist, we can *strike!*"

It was not long before the other men of the tribe did a wise thing. They ignored his descent from his Mahican mother, and decreed that he should be head chief of the Miamis. But Little

Turtle—as we will call him—was not content
with that. He sought the leadership of many
tribes and the command of thousands of warriors.
Thus, and thus only, could he accomplish his lifelong dream of driving out the white men.

In a neighboring tribe he found an able ally
in a young chief of about his own age—Bluejacket. He was a Shawnee of courage and re-
source, who enthusiastically seconded Little Turtle's scheme for a great confederation. Each of
them travelled widely through the country, visiting many tribes and pleading with them to drop
their petty squabbles and jealousies in the face of
this great common danger. How well they succeeded in uniting the tribes, the white command-
ers in the scattered army posts were soon to learn.

The founding of the town of Cincinnati was
one of the things which chiefly aroused the Indians' ire, as it lay directly in the trail leading
from north to south—from the hunting lands of
Ohio to those of Kentucky. It was likewise another obstacle on their beloved Ohio River. Two
companies of soldiers had come from Fort Harmar, near Marietta, to build a fort near the
mouth of the Little Miami River, which they
named Fort Washington, in honor of the President. It was a strong log structure with four
blockhouses commanding the corners—a grim

threat of war, and a daily reminder that the white man was here to seize the country for his own.

President Washington had had long experience with the Indians, and desired to keep on friendly terms with them. He instructed Harmar and St. Clair to exert every honorable effort to do this. They were told to buy the land from the natives and to respect their treaty rights. But the Indians refused to be mollified. They sat back on their haunches and said that he spoke with a forked tongue. When he tried to give them presents, they threw them on the ground. At the suggestion that they sell certain tracts to the white men, the scornful rejoinder was made:

"The Indian's lands are not for sale; they are his forever!"

Neither Bluejacket nor Little Turtle was present at this conference; they shrewdly remained in the background, but their scouts constantly reported its progress, and meanwhile they feverishly completed plans for beginning their war. By this time the confederation was a reality. Hundreds of warriors on both sides of the Ohio were only awaiting the signal to strike.

The white leaders were not ignorant of the gravity of the situation. They had long heard reports of the power of Little Turtle, and they saw that only a vigorous blow on their own part would upset his plans. They must strike first.

It was then the autumn of 1790. Fort Washington was completed and General Harmar had mustered an army of fourteen hundred men— no mean force for those days. It was their plan to march straight north into the heart of the Miami country, burning the villages and destroying the crops of corn and other supplies which the Indians had laid in for the winter. A simple and effective plan which would have crippled the Indians; but Harmar reckoned without the genius of Little Turtle. The first soldier had not set foot beyond the walls of the fort, before his scouts had told the chief of the force and its destination.

Northward the invaders marched for some miles, meeting with no opposition. The Indians fled before them, and their villages and crops went up in flames. The soldiers began to view the whole expedition as a lark—all, that is, except the old-timers.

Against the advice of these veterans, a small raiding party detached itself from the main force and started off on an expedition of its own. But unknown to themselves they were marching straight for the headquarters of Little Turtle. As they rode in careless unconcern through the forest, they found themselves suddenly surrounded by a horde of yelling Indians, commanded by a chief of fine physique who rode a pony, and had a single eagle feather in his scalp-lock.   It was Little Turtle himself.

So swift was the attack that in a very few minutes every member of the party was killed or taken prisoner, with the exception of a few mounted horsemen bringing up the rear.   Seeing that they were outnumbered, they turned and spurred their mounts back in the direction of the army.

Far from being disheartened by these tidings, General Harmar welcomed the fact that the Indian forces were so near.

"Forward, my men!" he shouted, cheerily. "We will surround these Miamis and cut them to pieces!"

He accordingly divided his army into two parts, which took opposite directions in a wide encircling movement.   The object was to engage the Indians with one force, and then spring a surprise attack upon them from the rear.   The plan might have been successful, had not an excited soldier forgotten his orders, on his first sight of the foe.   He fired his weapon and thus betrayed to Little Turtle the presence of the second body. Although caught between the two jaws of a pincer, like the able general that he was, he turned the situation to his own advantage.   With his ally, Bluejacket, commanding one wing of the Indian army, and himself the other, he threw himself fiercely at the first of the two American forces to engage him. Yelling like fiends, his men charged. Many of them were on ponies—a new mode of warfare for that section of the country, but so well did they ride that horse and man seemed a single creature.

The Americans were thrown into disorder by the ardor of their attack. Also, divided as they were, the Miamis outnumbered them. No sooner had Little Turtle accomplished his purpose in routing one force, than he turned swiftly and smote the other. General Harmar's men were totally unprepared for such a reception. They had been taught to believe that an Indian attack usually consisted of one sharp onslaught, then a retreat for a possible later attack. But Little Turtle fought more after the white man's style. His men gave no signs of quitting. Instead, they fought with desperate courage. They had been waiting for this moment for months and years, and they were commanded by two great chiefs.

General Harmar, also, was an able commander, and he strove desperately to reform his lines. But in their divided condition the men were demoralized, as the foe, screeching like demons, rode their wiry ponies back and forth in the shattered lines—some firing guns, others bows, and still others using spear and club. Soon the bugle sounded retreat, and the remnant of his army struggled back toward Fort Washington. It was a sorry ending to the foray which had started out so bravely a few days before; and it left the Indians more defiant and cocksure than ever.

Soon alarming reports began to filter in of renewed attacks upon the border forts and settlers. General St. Clair realized that a much larger expedition would have to be organized, in order to defeat the strongly entrenched Miamis. So he went across the Alleghenies to Philadelphia to consult with President Washington about it. Both recognized the gravity of the situation. Not only were the settlers already in the Ohio country not safe, but it was extremely dangerous for any others to attempt to go there. The Northwest Territory could never be settled until Little Turtle was defeated.

St. Clair was a veteran of the Revolution—a brave if not brilliant man. Washington, however, was more than this; he was an Indian fighter who had won his spurs as a young man even before the time of Braddock's disastrous defeat at the hands of the French and Indians on the way to Fort DuQuesne. Washington recalled those days to his war comrade, by way of caution. Laying his hand affectionately on St. Clair's shoulder, he said:

"Do not lay yourself open again to a surprise

attack. Remember that an Indian attacks always at the time you least expect it."

"I know that, your Excellency," replied St. Clair, gravely.

Armed with credentials from the President, he set actively to work raising a second army for the Ohio. The men were promised land in addition to other pay. It took a year to get the new force into shape, but by late summer of the year 1791 it was in evidence. There were two thousand men mustered in at Marietta—many of them frontiersmen and seasoned fighters. But others were recruits who had seen no Indian fighting. The little border town took on the aspect of a boom mining place in those busy days. Tents sprang up everywhere as if by magic. Flatboats by the score came down the river. Teams of horses and oxen struggled in dragging prairie schooners laden with supplies. One would have thought that the sight would strike terror to Little Turtle and his men, even if seen from afar. Although he doubtless knew every move that was made, he gave no sign.

When the white men discussed him, as they constantly did around their mess, it was to pooh-pooh the idea of any determined resistance to such an army. His defeat of Harmar's men they laid to luck and bad judgment. All *they*

wanted was a chance at the Miamis to even up
the score.

Their general made his plans thoroughly.
Knowing that an army "crawls on its stomach,"
he arranged to keep constant communication
with his base of supplies and to carry abundant
food and equipment with him. It was just a year
after the rout of Harmar when his army started
north. Again their object was to lay waste the
Indian country and if possible engage Little
Turtle himself. They were only afraid that the
wily chief would elude them.

On his march north, St. Clair stopped to build
two forts—Hamilton and Jefferson. They were
to serve as reserve posts and part of a permanent
defense against the Indians. The long line of
mounted and marching men moved slowly across
the prairie, reminding one of a gigantic snail.
They were, nevertheless, constantly on their
guard. Scouts rode ahead, and others protected
the rear. In open country like this it would be
hard for the Indians to stage an ambush.

Several days passed without any signs of Indians in force, and the men began to grow over-
confident. Little Turtle had been very much over-
estimated, they said. If he wanted to fight, now
was the time. But the body of scouts who accompanied them only looked the more grimly at
the peaceful skyline.

On the evening of the third of November (1791) they made camp for the night. It had been a long and tiring day; the going hard over the boggy, uneven country where they had to make their own trails. They had reached a place later called St. Mary's, on a branch of the Wabash. The general climbed wearily out of his saddle. He was getting well along in years, and an attack of gout was giving him trouble. His men, made up in part of regulars and in part of volunteers, did not work well together. Some of the latter were hardy woodsmen of independent spirit who resented any sort of leadership, especially on the part of a man who "had one foot in the grave," as they expressed it. They did so much grumbling that, when camp was pitched, they elected to stay in one spot, while the scouts and regulars stopped in another, a little way off.

The night seemed quiet and peaceful otherwise. Only the mournful hoot of an owl in the distance was heard. A light snow had begun to fall—the first of the season—and an occasional sentry pacing here and there was the only sign of life without the camp. But some of the old scouts were uneasy at the stillness, and considered going to the general and asking him to post extra men; but knowing the grumbling it would cause, especially on the part of the recruits, they did not do so.

The morning of the 4th began to dawn, clear and cold. Just as the first streaks of gray light shot across the sky, the report of a gun was heard, followed by the cry of a sentinel: "The Indians! the Indians!" Instantly it was followed by a pandemonium of shrieks and yells as out of the night came charging hundreds of men. They seemed to burst up out of the ground, so suddenly did they appear from all sides. They had, in fact, wriggled their way up with infinite cunning and caution until they were right upon the sentries before discovered.

It would be hard to describe the scene of confusion which followed. Imagine awaking out of a sound sleep to find Indian foes, hideously painted, yelling and striking down all whom they met! They were at such close quarters that few shots were fired. Knives, tomahawks, and clubs were the favorite weapons.

Although at a tremendous disadvantage the men sprang to their feet fighting. Grasping any weapon handy, and often with nothing save their bare hands, they engaged the enemy. In the briefest space of time the camp was transformed into a seething, writhing mass of humanity. Viewed in the half light of early morning it must have resembled a scene of the Inferno. Few shots were fired, as it would have been at the risk of hitting a friend as well as a foe. Here would be two stalwart figures, Indian and white soldier, locked in the embrace of death. There two others rolled over and over on the ground, biting, clawing, and scratching like wild cats. Again a single luckless soldier would be done to his death by the onslaught of three or four Indians at once.

The gradual brightening of day brought the scene out in all its horrors. More and more of the regulars were coming up to the support of the recruits. The scouts were trying to advance through the woods, fighting Indian-fashion from behind every bush and tree. Soon, however, they were forced to retreat. A large body of Indians were advancing, led by a man on horseback, who was surrounded by a picked bodyguard of braves. It was Little Turtle himself, come at last to answer the white man's challenge!

Under his terse orders his warriors ceased to fight in desultory fashion and began to charge again en masse, as they had done against Harmar. Springing back for a little space they gave the chance for other braves to discharge their guns and bows. Then they advanced in a body, while the Americans gave ground, though striving desperately to form and counter-charge.

And General St. Clair? Brave as his opponent, he was handicapped by physical disability.

Early in the mêlée he had been assisted into his saddle, and his shouts of "This way, men! Give them the bayonet!" might have been heard by those near by. He himself led an attack as soon as the light grew strong enough, and the nearest body of Indians was dislodged from among the trees—only to be reinforced by others. His horse was shot from under him, but another was quickly tendered. During the course of that long and bloody day—for the fighting continued all day long—he lost five horses, but was himself unwounded. As he watched the rout of his splendid army, he may have wished more than once that some merciful bullet or arrow would single him out.

Giving ground by inches, constantly pursued by a murderous fire, the white army fell back. Then the retreat became a rout and the way was strewn with the bodies of men and horses. For twenty-nine miles the gruesome trail led back to Fort Jefferson, and lucky indeed it was for them that they had this shelter to come to; for nearly one-half of that splendid force of two thousand men had been killed, wounded, or captured; while all their stores were lost. No such disaster had befallen an army at the hands of the Indians since the day of Braddock's Defeat. It had been the very disaster against which Washington had particularly warned St. Clair!

When the dreadful news was carried across the mountains, bringing sorrow to every town and hamlet in the East, and reached the President, he was overcome with grief and, at first, rage against St. Clair. Then pity for the old veteran took its place.

"Oh, why did he fall into this trap!" he exclaimed. "My warnings seem to fall on deaf ears. What a loss of good men! What shall we tell their families?"

But if deep sorrow was the portion of the white men, no less deep rejoicing was that of the Indians. Following the battle they had royal carnival. Each brave was staggering under his load of booty, and great was the feast which was held next day, presided over in state by Little Turtle and his allies headed by Bluejacket. Their day of vengeance had come, and to end its celebration fittingly a dreadful bonfire was lighted. Many of the helpless captives, some of them not able to stand on account of their wounds, were tied to stakes and burned. It was the Indian's way of taking toll for all his accumulated wrongs.

A war ballad of the times, written by the white men, has given us a graphic picture of St. Clair's Defeat. A closing stanza runs:

Alas, the dying and wounded, how dreadful was the
  thought!
To the tomahawk and scalping-knife in misery are
  brought.
Some had a thigh and some an arm broke on the field
  that day,
Who writhed in torments at the stake to close the dire
  affray.

For many months after this victory it seemed
to the Miamis that their dream had come true.
No more boats came down the Ohio; no more
prairie schooners toiled along over the land. The
cleared ground of the former settlers was revert-
ing back to wilderness. The Indian was coming
again into his own. But Little Turtle was not
misled by this fancied peace. He had scouts far
afield, and presently they began to bring to his
ears disquieting rumors. The white men were
raising a still larger army to bring into the Ohio
country. It was to be led by a famous veteran
of the Revolution whom they called "Mad Anthony" Wayne. He it was who had captured
Stony Point from the British, in a midnight
charge, ordering his men to use the bayonet to
conceal the fact that their guns were empty.

As Little Turtle and Bluejacket heard more
and more about this soldier and the size of his
force, they conferred together gravely. So many
tales were told of his prowess and watchfulness,

that the Indians dubbed him "The Black Snake," and "The Chief Who Never Sleeps."

Nearly three years passed by in this watchful waiting on both sides. Then to the chiefs came definite word that Wayne and his army had reached the borders of their country. For the first time in his career, Little Turtle had misgivings.

"I like it not," he confided to Bluejacket. "We can scarcely hope to surprise the foe a third time, and they outnumber our braves and have better weapons."

"Is my brother growing faint-hearted?" asked Bluejacket, with the faintest touch of sarcasm in his voice.

"Has my brother any cause to ask this?" retorted Little Turtle. "But the voice of caution is not the voice of the coward. One can win wars with the tongue."

"If we come to them with smooth words now, they will think us defeated indeed," insisted Bluejacket, impatiently.

"For my own life I care not a straw," continued Little Turtle, evenly; "but I cannot throw away the lives of my braves needlessly."

Thus they argued until dawn of a summer night, but without agreeing. Little Turtle was for conciliation and the making of an advantageous treaty of peace. From the many reports received concerning "The Chief Who Never Sleeps," and the size of his army, he saw only disaster to his people. The impetuous Bluejacket, however, was for taking the field.

On the next evening, at a council fire, they each in turn harangued the other leaders, and long and heated was the powwow. The final decision was for war. One strong reason for continuing to fight was their belief that the British soldiers would come to their aid and drive out the Americans.

"Our English father at the north only awaits the great day to strike," urged Bluejacket, cunningly.

"Our English father will stay in the northlands," replied Little Turtle, sagely.

Although this was some years after the close of the Revolution, the British had not relinquished all the border forts. They still held Detroit, among others, and put off evasively the time for its surrender. They even came down with a small force and built another fort to the south, in Ohio. It is not surprising, therefore, that the Indians still looked to them for aid. The attitude of the British misled the Indians and drove them to further warfare, thus delaying for many years the settlement of the Northwest Territory.

"We will retreat before 'The Black Snake,'

and lure him on to the posts of our English brothers," insisted Bluejacket. "Then with their help we will drive these hated Yankees out of our country forever."

This speech was wildly applauded by the others—especially by the young braves who itched to get their first scalps at their belts. For a warrior did not amount to much in the eyes of his tribe or among the maidens until he had won these bloody trophies.

"So be it!" consented Little Turtle at last. "I shall be with my braves when the cry of battle shrills in the air."

Came the day when the first of the white scouts were reported, in advance of the army. The scouts may have thought themselves undetected as they stole along, but every move was reported to the wary chief.

Up on the northern trail—the same that had been taken by the unlucky St. Clair—advanced Wayne and his men. They were tanned, grizzled, and determined looking. Their equipment was light and they travelled fast. In a few days they had reached the scene of St. Clair's Defeat without firing a shot. They had stopped on the way only to destroy some of the Indians' fields of standing corn, or a village. But the Indians themselves kept out of the way and joined the main army of braves in the north.

At the scene of the former bloody battle, Wayne found a heap of charred human bones— mute evidence of the sacrifice which had followed the defeat. He reverently gathered them up and buried them. A fort was built at the spot, which he called Fort Recovery.

Still there was no sign of the Indians; but Wayne was not misled. He was matching his wits against one of the shrewdest of Indian leaders, and he did not intend to be caught napping. Steadily he marched on northward, but so cautiously that Little Turtle saw it would be useless to try to lure him into an ambush or surprise him by a night attack. The advancing host was now within a few miles of Lake Erie, near the Maumee River, and only a short distance away from the British stronghold.

Near the junction of the Maumee and the Auglaize rivers they found many deserted huts and large fields of corn—showing that they had reached the headquarters of the Miamis. Still there was no hostile move, and the frontier army were glad to replenish their own stores of food, before destroying the fields. A fort was built here, called "Defiance," and Wayne sent scouts ahead to Little Turtle, with a final offer of peace. Firm in the belief that the British would help them, the other chiefs advised him to refuse. When this answer was received, Wayne moved his troops down the left bank of the Maumee toward the British fort.

Facing 'this crisis, Little Turtle elected to choose his own battle-ground. A storm had thrown down some trees, on a wooded knoll, and he set his braves to work felling others and forming them into a rampart. Lying prone behind these logs—their muskets primed and ready— the Indians, a thousand strong, awaited the approach of the frontiersmen.

When Wayne's scouts reported this situation to him, he saw that some hard fighting was ahead. The only way to dislodge the foe was by charging through these fallen timbers, in the face of a thousand guns, and as many more knives and tomahawks. Like St. Clair, Wayne had fallen a victim to the gout, and after several days in the saddle he had become so crippled that he could hardly walk. But as they neared the Indian line, the excitement nerved him to forget his own disability. He had his men lift him from the horse, and he charged with them on foot, straight for the barricade.

"Drive them out, men!" he ordered.

With a yell of defiance matching the Indians' own, the soldiers dashed forward. Little Turtle, Bluejacket, and the other chiefs held their men in leash until the soldiers were almost upon them —then they gave the order to fire. A thousand guns spat forth flame, and here and there an onrushing figure dropped. The rest, nevertheless, came straight on, not giving the Indians time to reload.

"Make war-clubs of your guns!" yelled Little Turtle.

"Give them cold steel!" commanded Wayne, on his side.

In the fierce hand-to-hand fighting which ensued, few orders were given or heeded. It was each man for himself, but from the outset the Indians were at a disadvantage. They were outnumbered and they grew confused. As they turned to flee, the soldiers fired their own weapons, turning the battle into a rout. In vain, Little Turtle, Bluejacket, and other chiefs tried to re-form their lines. But the tide of war had already turned against the Indians. Now they ran away so fast that the ground was strewn with their weapons and clothes. They fled almost up to the walls of the British fort, but its gates did not open to them, nor did a single redcoat come out to assist them. It is not known how many they lost, although it was much greater than the American loss, which was thirty-three killed and one hundred wounded.

The engagement, which was short and decisive, was known ever after as the Battle of Fallen Timbers. It brought a cessation of hostilities to that troubled land, which lasted for eighteen years. It also convinced the British that for them it was "time to retire."

General Wayne promptly followed up his victory by building a chain of forts from north to south right through the heart of the Indian country. The one at the junction of the St. Mary's and St. Joseph rivers was named Fort Wayne, in his honor, and was the site of the later prosperous city.

Meanwhile, in the lodges of the Indians was much sorrow. They realized, too late, the wisdom of Little Turtle's counsel. Had they treated for peace earlier, they might have made a good bargain. Now they must take any crust that the victor threw at them. To all their overtures of peace, he gave no answer other than the curt, "Meet me at Greenville." Thus for several months he kept them on the anxious seat—as he desired—and he also ensured a full attendance of all the warring tribes. This must be no patched-up peace, he reasoned; it must be with all the tribes and for all time.

With the summer of 1795, the fields and woods round about Greenville presented a crowded and motley appearance. At least a thousand Indians were present. Here were the Miamis; there the Shawnees; yonder the Kickapoos, the Ottawas, the Wyandots, the Iroquois, the Chippewas, the

Pottawatomies, the Cahokias, the Kaskaskias, and a score of others. They had had enough of war. They were ready to make peace, although they realized sadly that it must be at the expense of the very things they had fought for so long—their homes and hunting grounds.

Came the day of the opening of the council, and "The Chief Who Never Sleeps" strode forward and confronted the circle of braves, seated sullenly upon the ground in a semi-circle. They made no sound as he paused and looked in first one face and then another. Knowing their fondness for speaking in symbols, he held up the shield of the United States for all to see. There was the American eagle, clutching in its talons a sheaf of arrows.

"Our eagle never sleeps," said Wayne, impressively. "His eye is keen and unwavering; he looks the sun in the eye without blinking. When he strikes"—pointing to the clutched arrows—"he brings death to many warriors. You yourselves know this. But see"—he added, pointing to the olive branch which the eagle also clutched, —"the American eagle brings peace as well as war. Which will you choose?"

There could be but one answer, although the warriors deliberated some days before they gave it. "Peace!" they said, and made their marks haltingly upon the official paper which Wayne spread before them.

Little Turtle had taken scant part in the council. His heart was heavy as he saw the confederation, to which he had given his whole life, thus dissipated into thin air. He sat back haughtily, his blanket wrapped about him, and witnessed one after another of his allies go forward and sign the treaty. When there was none left except himself, Wayne looked at him inquiringly. Little Turtle rose and came forward, slowly and proudly. He seized the pen and wrote his own name—his Indian one—upon the document. Then he turned to General Wayne and said:

"I am the last to sign it, and I will be the last to break it."

The sober pages of history state that he kept his word. He counseled his people against further war from that time to the day of his death, in 1812—seventeen years after this treaty was signed.

History also gives us another scene from this Indian hero's life—a pleasant one. Two years after the Treaty of Greenville, he went by invitation to Philadelphia, where he met the Great Father—Washington himself. The latter was deeply interested in him and chatted with him in most friendly style about Indian affairs; promising on his part to see that their rights were respected.

Little Turtle also met other military leaders, including the famous General Kosciusko, who presented him with a pair of elegantly mounted pistols. He sat for his portrait to the celebrated painter, Gilbert Stuart, whose Washington portraits are so well known. Little Turtle's likeness is that of an Indian of regular features and remarkably high forehead—a man born to command.

He passed away in peaceful old age, respected by his own race and the white one alike—a man who had given his life for a cause, whose sagacity equalled his courage, and whose word was his bond.

CHAPTER TEN

TECUMSEH AND THE PROPHET

"BUT I tell you, my brother, that all this land belongs to the Indian!"

"Then why does he allow the pale-face forts at every river fork?" retorted the other.

Two Indian lads were engaged in earnest debate, as they sat on the banks of an Ohio stream. It was not the first of such conversations by any means, and it was but an echo of what fell from the lips of the men around the council fire. They had crept up as close as they dared, to overhear these impassioned discussions.

"Did you hear what Shawman the Truth Teller said last night?" asked the older of the boys, a well-set-up youth of fourteen or fifteen. "Shawman is very old and very wise. He must have seen a hundred summers and winters. He remembers the day when the Indian could hunt the buffalo and bear and deer from the Alleghenies at the east, to the Father of Waters in the west. The only white men here were the French, who were our brothers. And you have heard him tell of Pontiac, the great chief, whose

196

name was feared from Michilimackinac and Detroit down to Kentucky. Would that those great days could come again!"

"They can, Tecumseh, if you and I and the other young braves of to-morrow will go again on the warpath. Are we squaws that we are not to have a single scalplock on our belts?"

"You may well ask, Tenskwatawa, but remember the fate of our father. He fought with the great chief, Cornstalk, at the Battle of Point Pleasant, and lost his life there. And one after another, his brothers have fallen. Our own brother was slain last year down in Kentucky. What then can the Indian do but submit—or be slain?"

"It is not like you to talk thus, Tecumseh," said the other. "As for me, when I am grown, I am going to be an orator. I shall go from village to village speaking to the braves—telling them of our past glories and urging them to stand firm. I shall be a prophet!"

"And so shall I," retorted Tecumseh. "But I shall do more than talk—I shall fight!"

Tecumseh and his brother, Tenskwatawa, were Shawnees, living in the tribal village of Piqua. Their village has long since ceased to exist, but near its site is now the thriving city of Springfield, Ohio. Every Indian name signifies something. "Tecumseh" meant "one who crosses, or travels." He was destined to travel widely, and he was known later as the "Crouching Panther," and the "Shooting Star." Tenskwatawa meant "Out in the Open," or "Loud Voice." The chance·to fight, for which he yearned, finally came to the young Tecumseh. A scout bearing a red tomahawk hurried one day into their village with tidings that Little Turtle was on the warpath. He had determined to make a stand against the enemy, and was summoning his braves from every tribe for many miles to assist him. Eagerly Tecumseh and his friends responded to this call. When the braves gathered for their final rendezvous before the battle, there were warriors present from a score of tribes. The plains seemed alive with them. Two thousand or more had gathered around the banner of Little Turtle.[1] They were going against General St. Clair, a veteran of the Revolution, who, with a picked force of two thousand men, was marching north into the Ohio country. Little Turtle, however, proved the abler general, and in a surprise attack, totally defeated the white army. Nearly half of St. Clair's men were slain, and the rest scattered in headlong flight.

Tecumseh got his first taste of real battle that day, and his eyes gleamed with fine scorn as he watched the retreat of St. Clair's shattered com-

[1] See story of "Little Turtle and the Miamis."

panies. This was in the year 1791, and for
months thereafter the Indians roamed at will
over their regained country, and the question of
white settlement looked remote indeed. But
meanwhile another general in the East was busily
recruiting an army to avenge St. Clair's defeat—
"Mad Anthony" Wayne, the hero of more than
one spirited exploit in the Revolution. He
brought a still larger army into the Ohio country
and defeated Little Turtle decisively at the Battle of Fallen Timbers.

Tecumseh, now a brave in the early twenties,
fought courageously in this battle. A brother
was slain by his side, but he himself escaped without a wound. He had gained a new respect for
the arms of the Americans, but his heart was
filled with a still deeper hatred. He resolved
to devote his life to the regaining of the lands
of his people.

When the American commissioners came to
treat with the Indians for the purchase of lands
from certain tribes, he stubbornly held aloof.
"This country belongs to all the tribes in common," he said. "No single tribe has the right to
part with it. We will never sell it!"

Despite his protests, he saw more and more
white-covered wagons coming across the mountains from the east, and a flotilla of flatboats
breasting the wide current of the Ohio, each and

all bringing settlers into the territory. More than one desperate fight was waged by lurking Indians for the possession of one of these flat-boats, and at times the intrepid frontiersmen lost their lives in the encounter. But still others came to take their places.

Tecumseh, who had been gaining increased authority and prestige, now bestirred himself. He had visions of a great confederation which should extend from the Great Lakes to the Gulf, and present a united front against the invaders. Filled with this idea he went in person from one tribe to another, travelling hundreds of miles, even as far south as Florida, and as far west as the Missouri River. He was a natural orator and a man who would command attention anywhere. When he stood up by the council fire to speak, there was instant silence, for his hearers instinctively realized the leadership of the man. Here was a great chief, one whom they had long awaited, come at last.

For years he perfected his plans and built his widespread confederation, but so quietly that, as usual, the white men knew nothing of the danger. Beyond an occasional local trouble the Indians were peaceful, and the settlement of Ohio and Indiana had gone forward rapidly. The white men began to estimate the power and rights of their Indian friends cheaply, and it is probable that they would have fallen victims to the same widespread attack so successfully engineered by Pontiac of old, had it not been for the vainglory of one man—the "Prophet."

The younger brother of Tecumseh was achieving his own boyhood ambition of being a great orator. He was living up to his Indian name, Tenskwatawa, meaning "Out in the Open," and "Loud Voice." Either title fitted, as he was always much in evidence, and liked to hear the sound of his own voice. He called himself a prophet sent by the Great Spirit to show the true way to his people. He abjured them to give up the white man's ways and return to their ancient virtues. He told them to leave "fire-water" alone, as it was a poison used by the white men to take away the Indian's strength—and in this he was right. He preached against witchcraft and the medicine juggleries of his tribe, and urged them not to wreak vengeance on their enemies by torture. So we see that much of his preaching was laudable.

"Do not intermarry with the white men," he exhorted them. "Do not wear their clothes or ape their manners. Do not so much as make fire by their methods. Return to the ways of your fathers and thus will you receive strength to drive the hated paleface from your possessions.

"As for me," he continued, smiting himself

upon the chest, "I am your Prophet. I am sent to you by the Great Spirit. I am bullet-proof. No harm can come to me on the field of battle —and no harm to you likewise, if you follow me!"

Or at another time he would say: "Are you dogs, that you should slink away when the white man approaches? Are you squaws? If you are men, follow me! The Great Spirit commands it!"

By such speeches as this he began to stir up the more truculent element and to gather to himself a considerable following. With his growing power he became more boastful than ever. His boasts finally came to the ears of the governor of the territory, General William Henry Harrison, who later became President. The governor sent out scouts, who reported that the Prophet was more of a wind-bag than a warrior, but that his brother, Tecumseh, was a chieftain to be respected. He, they said, was rumored to be the head of a great and growing confederation.

General Harrison decided that the promptest action was necessary to nip this plot in the bud. He accordingly sent emissaries to invite the two brothers to a conference. The wily Prophet pleaded excuses and would not parley. But Tecumseh came, with four hundred warriors, and called upon the governor, in the little frontier town of Vincennes. When confronted with the charge that he had been plotting against the white men, he replied with great native eloquence that he was not answerable to any other nation for his actions. He was trying to protect his own people from the injustice of the invaders.

"You come into Indian country," he cried passionately, "and drive us out to make room for your own towns and farms. And when we try to stand firm, you accuse us of plotting against you!" Then he went on to recite some of the grievances of his people.

When he had ended and still stood glaring defiance, one of General Harrison's aides stepped forward and said to him: "Your father requests you to take a seat by his side."

Tecumseh only drew his blanket the more tightly about him, and looked coldly at the speaker.

"My father!" he repeated. "The sun is my father, and the earth my mother. On her breast I will repose!"

Thus saying, he seated himself upon the ground.

General Harrison saw that, with Tecumseh in this frame of mind, it was idle to try to smoke the pipe of peace with him. He contented himself with answering Tecumseh's complaints, and assuring him that the settlers wished to live on friendly terms with the Indian chiefs. But Tecumseh only grunted scornfully, and soon departed with his warriors.

With the Indians in this threatening attitude, the warning went forth to all the colonists to be on their guard. More blockhouses were built, and every cabin was zealously guarded against a surprise attack. More than one such attack was made on some lonely cabin, and soon the whole border was tense with anxiety. Then came word that Tecumseh was again in the south, stirring up the Seminoles and others against the Americans. Meanwhile, the Prophet went strutting about in Ohio and Indiana, haranguing all who would listen and making the most extravagant boasts.

The governor resolved to end this menace by striking the first blow. If war must come, he preferred to pick his own time and place. Mustering an army of several hundred expert riflemen, he marched north toward the Indian village on the Tippecanoe, where the Prophet had his headquarters. It was in the autumn of 1811, and there had been reports that British agents from Canada were also active with the Indians, trying to stir them up, in view of a possible war with the United States—a war which was, in fact, to break out the next year. So it was doubly desirable to break the power of the Indians without delay.

The Prophet had an army of at least a thousand men, and was no mean antagonist, as Harrison well knew. He also knew of the Indian's tricky nature. He was not surprised, therefore, when on nearing the chief's village, the Prophet himself came out to meet him, with a small company of his warriors.

"Why does my father march against us in this warlike manner?" asked the wily Prophet.

"Why do your braves lay waste the country-side?" demanded General Harrison, sternly.

"They are not acting under any orders of mine," the chief replied. "But let us not quarrel. Let us smoke the pipe of peace and friendship. Give me till to-morrow's sun, and we will hold council and I will do anything you say."

So profuse was he in his offers of peace, that the governor agreed to wait until the morrow for a further parley. He would not enter the Indian village, he said, but would pitch his camp where he stood. His men had marched all day and were glad of the chance to cook their supper and get some sleep. But he himself was not deluded by the Prophet's tongue. He knew this Indian of old and suspected that he was trying to gain time for his own ends. He warned his men to be extra vigilant that night, to guard against surprise.

The night was cloudy and dark, with threatened rain. Fires were built in many parts of the camp, and while the sentry watched the surrounding bushes with keen eyes, the tired men took turns in sleeping, but each man with his gun lying ready at his side.

Slowly the hours dragged by in absolute quiet save for the hooting of some restless owl, which was answered by another from the opposite wood. Just before dawn when night was at its blackest and it seemed that the whole world was in slumber, an arrow whizzed from a thicket striking a sentinel in the throat. He gave a gurgle, threw up his hands, fell forward and lay still. A moment later another fell victim to this silent messenger of death. But a comrade saw him fall and instantly gave the alarm. As he shouted, a shower of arrows came hurtling through the air and in a moment every thicket seemed alive with Indians. Forward they dashed, yelling like madmen, brandishing their tomahawks and making for the center of the camp.

Despite their precautions the army was taken by surprise. The men woke up in a daze with the Indians right upon them. But they were not green troops; most of them had fought Indians before. It was partly instinct which brought them to their feet fighting. They grabbed their guns as a matter of habit, and where they had no time to fire them, used them as clubs upon the nearest enemy's head. A scene of indescribable confusion followed. The entire camp was a vortex of struggling figures and in the half light of the fires it was hard to distinguish friend from foe. Here would be a struggling group of four or five, clutching at each other's throats, tearing at the scalplocks, or clubbing right and left indiscriminately. Yonder two stalwart figures would be grimly locked in the embrace of death. An occasional shot rang out, but more often it was the flash of a knife or tomahawk, or the thud of a club which told of the intensity of the conflict.

After the first shock of surprise the Indians no longer had the advantage. They found the white men meeting them man to man and more than holding their own. An Indian's favorite method of fighting is by sudden attack and just as sudden retreat. He thinks it no shame to fall back and pick the time for his next foray. He does not attempt sustained fighting—and this was what he got in the dim haze of early morning here on the banks of the Tippecanoe.

Meanwhile, what of the Prophet—he of the bullet-proof skin? He had taken good care that this claim should not be put to the acid test. He had not mingled in the mélee, but stood apart on a little mound exhorting his men to stand firm and, by turns, calling upon the Great Spirit to aid him in battle. He danced up and down; he yelled and screeched; he waved his arms; he made all the "medicine" that he knew how to make; but not once did he get in range of the fighting.

As for General Harrison, he was on his feet at the first alarm. A party of Indians had made for his tent but were beaten off. He fought alongside of his men, for, indeed, few orders could be issued at first. It was every man for himself. But as day began to dawn, his voice could be heard above the din:

"Fall in, men! This way! Give them a volley of lead!"

Discipline told over the untrained Indian. The men began to form into squads and companies. Their assailants recoiled and fled. With broad daylight they were in full retreat in every direction, and the Prophet was nowhere to be seen. He had made an inglorious exit.

"After them!" was the general's curt order, and the men with ringing cheers obeyed. They were smarting to get even with the enemy for his attack in the dark. For miles they pursued them, cutting down fugitives all along the way. The village at Tippecanoe was totally destroyed with a large amount of stores—a serious blow to the Indians. The American loss had been heavy— sixty or more killed and twice as many wounded

—but the Indian loss had been much heavier. Their power was completely broken.

The Prophet had remained bullet-proof simply because he had kept out of range of the bullets, but he was disgraced and discredited in the eyes of his people. It was worse than any bodily wound. When his brother, the great Tecumseh, heard of this defeat he hurried north and bitterly reproached him for hastening the conflict before his own plans were ripe. Naught remained for him but to conclude a treaty of peace with the triumphant Americans, and at their terms. Tecumseh, however, still nursed an undying hatred in his heart for the Americans and only bided his time to strike another blow.

It came with the outbreak of the War of 1812 between England and the United States. As soon as this news came to him, he hastened to Canada and offered his services to the British general. They were gladly accepted and he was made a brigadier general in the British army. He recruited two thousand braves for his own command and again his name struck terror into the settlers. The northern parts of Ohio and Indiana, and the whole peninsula of Michigan were soon overrun with his men. The post at Mackinaw speedily surrendered before a force of British and Indians, as there were only about sixty men in this garrison.

Down at Detroit, the key point which Pontiac had besieged so vainly a few years before, the British, aided by Tecumseh, again had an easy conquest. General Hull, the American commander, grew faint-hearted when he saw the waters in front of his fort full of boats flying the Union Jack, and his scouts had reported the near presence of Tecumseh at his rear. Although he had a strong force and plenty of stores at the time, he hauled down his flag without firing a shot.

General Winchester, another veteran of the Revolution, was placed at the head of the American forces in the north, after Hull's surrender, but disaster likewise followed his arms. He joined forces with Colonel Lewis in Michigan, the combined army numbering about nine hundred. In January, 1813, on the banks of the River Raisin, they encountered a force of British and Indians, of about eleven hundred. The Americans were defeated, and Winchester was captured. His troops were surrendered as prisoners of war, on condition that they were not to be molested by the Indians. The English General, Proctor, agreed to this, and transferred all the unwounded prisoners across the river to Malden, Canada. The wounded men, however, were left behind under insufficient guard. The Indians fell upon and brutally massacred them. The deed sent a thrill of horror through the frontier, and "Remember the River Raisin!" became a battle-cry. Proctor himself came in for a great deal of the blame for this, but Tecumseh was not present. The Indian chief was averse to torture, and in other engagements forbade unnecessary bloodshed.

Flushed with his victories at the north, Proctor marched south to conquer Ohio and the other colonies, bringing with him the redoubtable Tecumseh. But now they found a foe worthy of their steel. Harrison and his Kentuckians awaited them. He was entrenched at Fort Meigs, at the Maumee Rapids, in northwestern Ohio, where he had elected to meet the enemy after hearing the dire news of the bloody massacre of the River Raisin. Harrison had a force which was not one-third that of the English and Indians, but every man had resolved to fight to the last. When Proctor sent a demand for the surrender of the fort, Harrison replied:

"Tell General Proctor that, if he shall take the fort, it will be under circumstances that will do him more honor than a thousand surrenders."

The plucky Americans resisted every attack and strategy on the part of both Proctor and Tecumseh, the siege lasting ten days. Then the opportune arrival of General Green Clay with

American reinforcements turned the tide, and Proctor withdrew.

Another brilliant defense of an American position came a few weeks later. Fort Stephenson, a weak stockade mounting only a single six-pound gun, lay directly in Proctor's path. It was commanded by a young Irish-Kentuckian named Croghan, who had about one hundred and sixty men, all told. Harrison ordered him to save himself by evacuating the position; but Croghan decided to risk a court-martial for insubordination, and hold it. Hold it he did against unbelievable odds. He shifted his one six-pounder from one part of the parapet to another, to give the impression of a battery. Proctor ordered him to surrender, telling him that he himself would not be able to hold back his Indian allies, if the fort were taken by storm. Croghan defied him to do his worst, and yelled: "Remember the River Raisin!"

The British then attacked in earnest, choosing the weakest side of the stockade. Here, however, they encountered the deadly fire of the Kentucky riflemen, who never believed in wasting ammunition. Scores of the British fell before they reached the moat on the outer side of the stockade. Still other brave redcoats took their places and began to chop an opening through the timbers. Again the faithful six-pounder spoke. It had been filled with slugs and pointed directly at the opening. At its terrible discharge the entire ditch was filled with dead and wounded men. The rest of the attacking party hastily drew off and made no more sorties that night.

Meanwhile, Croghan's men inside the fort were oppressed by the moans of the wounded lying just without.

"We must do something for them, men," ordered the commander.

They did not dare to open the gate to bring the wounded foe inside, but in the darkness they let down buckets of water from the tops of the walls, which some of the less injured managed to pass to the others. Next an opening was made just large enough to bring them in, a man at a time, and they were cared for as solicitously as though they had been patriots. When Tecumseh heard of this action, he got still another lesson in the way white men of the better breed fought. Another famous saying of General Harrison's doubtless came to his ears:

"Kentuckians, remember the River Raisin! But remember it only while victory is suspended. The revenge of a soldier can not be gratified upon a fallen enemy."

As for the reckless Croghan, he successfully beat off the enemy and held his little fort. His superior officer did not have the heart to discipline him severely for his disobedience to orders.

So long as the British controlled the Great Lakes, they held the key to the entire Northwest. The Americans realized this, and prepared to fight it out with them here as well. A British fleet under Barclay patrolled Lake Erie and protected Detroit. A young American naval officer, Oliver Hazard Perry, was sent from Philadelphia up through Ohio to recruit a force and build ships to meet him. The story of this adventure of shipbuilding and manning here on the frontier deserves a chapter to itself. Despite almost insuperable obstacles, the ships were launched and outfitted, and one bright day in September, 1813, the British commander saw a fleet nearly the size of his own, bravely flaunting the stars and stripes.

At the western end of the lake the two fleets came together. Early in the action Perry's flagship was riddled by the enemy's shot, but amid a hail of bullets Perry got into a small boat and transferred his flag to another vessel. The contest was bitterly and bravely waged on both sides, but the superior marksmanship of the Americans finally prevailed. The enemy's sails were cut to pieces by charges of slugshot, and one after another they were compelled to haul down their flags. At the close of this eventful day Perry was enabled to pen his memorable despatch to Congress:

"We have met the enemy and they are ours. Two ships, two brigs, one schooner, and one sloop."

Perry's brilliant victory put fresh heart into the patriot forces and also opened the way to Harrison and his men to retake Detroit. As he marched north and Tecumseh's scouts brought word of this advance, the cowardly Proctor grew as uncomfortable in his turn, as General Hull had been. Tecumseh witnessed his preparations for speedy flight with amazement and scorn.

"The Great Father"—the Indians' name for the King of England—"has given you arms and ammunition," he said. "If you are not going to use them, give them to his Indian allies—then you may go and welcome. Our lives are in the hands of the Great Spirit. We are determined to defend our lands and our homes, and if it be His will, we wish to leave our bones upon them!"

General Proctor, however, was deaf to the Indian's reproaches. Intent on saving his own skin —for he knew of the hatred which some of his brutal measures had aroused—he hauled down the Union Jack without firing a shot and crossed the river into Canada. Tecumseh followed him with rage and despair in his breast. He knew that unsupported he was no match for the American forces. His warriors while brave were undisciplined. Further, he himself was a general in the British army and must obey orders. Now, all that he could do was to cover the retreat of the British.

Harrison, after taking Detroit, lost no time in pursuing his enemy. Colonel Richard Johnson with a force of mounted Kentuckians dashed on ahead, and caught up with the fleeing redcoats near the present town of Chatham, on the River Thames. The fight which followed is known to history as the Battle of the Thames.

Tecumseh's scouts had kept him fully advised of the progress of the pursuing army. He saw that they must make a stand, and so informed Proctor. The latter reluctantly consented, although the two forces were about equal —some twenty-five hundred each. It is true that Proctor's force was largely Indian, but as the day proved, they were worthier antagonists than their white allies.

Proctor elected to meet the enemy in open formation, and seeing this wide extended line, the cavalry under Johnson dashed through the center and doubling back threw the whole line into confusion. Proctor, still afraid of the vengeance of those who shouted, "Remember the Raisin!" had no heart for fighting and thought only of his personal safety. He fled precipitately, first by carriage, then taking to the woods like a common fugitive. He reached Montreal, but only later to face a court-martial and the obloquy of his country.

And what of Tecumseh, his loyal ally? The great chieftain fell early in the battle—'tis said, by the sword of Johnson. But he fell with his face to the foe and fighting bravely to the last. He seems to have had a presentiment that this was to be his last fight, for before it began he took off the uniform of a British general, which he had worn with much pride and in which he had appeared a handsome and impressive figure. Laying all these trappings aside, he dressed himself as before in the simple deerskin leggings of an Indian brave, with naked, painted chest, and the single tall feather of a Shawnee chief in his scalplock. It was as an Indian and in the cause of his own people that he wished to meet the foe.

"Be strong, my braves!" he challenged, striding up and down the line. "Show these palefaces—friend and foe alike—how an Indian can die!"

And show them they did. The official records of the battle state that the only active resistance was made by the Indian forces under Tecumseh. But before the charging horses of the cavalry, and the deadly marksmanship of the frontiersmen, they were thrown into disorder. When they saw their chief go down, they fled. Tecumseh himself fell in the forefront of the battle, meeting, as he wished, the death of a warrior. To his indomitable spirit, death was preferable to witnessing the bondage of his people.

CHAPTER ELEVEN

OSCEOLA, THE SEMINOLE CHIEFTAIN

GENERAL WILEY THOMPSON, the government agent to the Indians, was at his wit's end—and all because of a stubborn young brave. He had called a parley of the Indians, down in one of the verdant groves of Florida, and had placed before them a treaty to sign, and this defiant warrior had balked at signing it.

Some two hundred and fifty of the Seminoles had gathered together in this semi-tropical spot, shaded by its live oaks, palms, and cypress, and redolent with magnolia and other Southern blossoms. It was a scene of wild, luxuriant beauty. The Indians knew and loved it as their home for many generations—and that is why the young brave stood defiant, when the commissioner urged him to sign the paper—for it meant the giving up of their home land.

General Thompson urged the move adroitly. He pictured the new lands far to the west, across the mighty river called the Father of Waters. There, he said, the Seminoles of Florida would be given broader lands and more suited to cultivation. They would find a new home in many respects better than this, and would dwell in peace forever. The Great Father at Washington was mindful of the welfare of the Seminoles, and that was why he sought to remove them from Florida.

"If the new lands to the west are so much better than these, why does not the Great Father send his white children there and leave us in peace?" countered the young chief, Osceola by name.

"You are young; you talk like a fool," sneered Enematkla, another Seminole, who was secretly in the pay of the white men. "See—I will sign the paper!"

And with a flourish he stepped up to the stout oak table on which lay the document, and made his cross-mark at the proper place. Following his example, a few other braves also affixed their cross-marks.

"It is sign this, or fight all the rest of our lives," they muttered to each other in their own tongue.

Osceola overheard them and his eye flashed fire. Drawing a dagger from his hunting shirt, he stepped forward and with a powerful stroke drove it through the paper and deep into the plank underneath.

"There is my mark!" he said.

The time of this dramatic scene was the year 1835, and in order to grasp its significance, let us glance back at a few of the events leading up to it.

Over a hundred years before, the Florida Indians, partially civilized by the Spaniards and living at peace with them, were raided by a large force of fierce Creeks from the north. At their head was Governor Moore, of the Carolinas, and his army of a thousand Creeks and English swooped suddenly down into the peaceful country, killing all the natives who withstood them, laying waste orange groves and plantations, destroying villages and missions, and, in short, uprooting the civilization of a hundred years, in a few days. Over two hundred Apalachee warriors were slain in battle, and fourteen hundred men, women and children were carried into slavery.

For many years after this dire fate, the lands lay open and untenanted; then another tribe took possession. They had been driven from their homes by the war, and at first skulked in the swamps and made only furtive efforts to till the soil. So the Creeks called them Seminoles, which means "runaways" or "wanderers," and contemptuously left them alone. In fact, it was easier to ignore them than to try to track them through the wild tangle of the Everglades.

This was the origin of the Seminole tribe, which in years to come became more and more powerful, finally forming an alliance with the Spaniards, and giving the American government much concern. At the close of the Revolution it is estimated that they had as many as twenty towns and roamed at will over the entire peninsula. Spain still owned Florida and she made use of the natives as political pawns for her own ends. During the War of 1812 the Seminoles became so troublesome that General Andrew Jackson led a fighting force of volunteers from Tennessee, to drive out the British and their allies. He took Pensacola by storm, successfully defended Mobile, and then marched west to win the brilliant victory over the British at New Orleans.

All the foregoing is a matter of history, but must be given, in order to follow the later fortunes of the Seminoles with any clearness.

Indians do not serve as pawns willingly. The Seminoles were no exception. They were shrewd enough to see that they were being used by first one side and then another. Their old men told them tales of the long ago, when they had been fugitives and wanderers. "Stand against these white men from the north," they counselled, "or again you will be driven out shelterless." The Spanish, also, cunningly advised them to fight, as this was the last of the Spanish possessions upon the northern continent. The result was the First Seminole War, as it is called, which broke out in 1817, and lasted for two years, until Spain ceded the territory to the United States. Again it was Jackson who brought victory to the Americans. Leading an army of three thousand men, his old fighting volunteers of Tennessee, with other Southerners, he pursued his campaign so relentlessly that the Seminoles were glad to sue for peace. By the Treaty of 1823, made at Fort Moultrie, they reluctantly parted with most of their lands, excepting a large central reservation.

However, like most treaties made between the races, this one was of short duration. White settlers came across the borders in such numbers that the government decided to transplant the entire tribe to lands across the Mississippi River. A treaty to this effect was negotiated in 1832— only nine years after—and the luckless Seminoles were given three years in which to "get out."

Anyone who loves his native land deeply can hardly fail to understand what such a move would mean to a people. The poet Longfellow immortalized the Acadians, in "Evangeline," for a similar fate. Like the Acadians, the only home the Seminoles had ever known was to be rudely snatched from them, and they were to be sent out to a land of strangers. Such was the doom visited upon the Seminoles, and it is small wonder that they resisted. General Thompson was sent down again in 1835 to compel them to sign the treaty giving up their land, and with the aid of the cunning Enematkla was succeeding well with it—when the unyielding Osceola interposed.

Osceola was then about thirty years old—a warrior who would attract attention in any throng. He had white blood in his veins, and some of the early writers say that he was the son of a Scotch trader by the name of Powell; others, that Powell was only his foster father, but that a grandfather was a white man. His mother, a full-blooded Creek, Cuspa by name, was the daughter of a chief. The boy grew up to be a comely and daring young woodsman. There was as little danger of his getting lost in the forest, as a buck. He was equally at home in the woods night or day. Sometimes in the ardor of the chase he would go until the stars were out, but he had come to know them and he found his way home as unerringly as though the sun were shining. He could climb up into the topmost branches of a live-oak, swinging from one limb to another and chattering laughingly back at the squirrels who scolded at the intruder on their domain.

When Osceola was grown he wooed and won a beautiful girl of a neighboring tribe, Ouskaloosa by name. Some legends are to the effect that he ran away with her and wedded her despite her people. He built a lodge on the banks of a small stream, and there they lived for a few years quite happily; she tilling a little garden; he hunting and fishing along the river.

But their happiness was not for long. As he came and went, he met other braves who told of the white men and how they were taking more and more of the land, and were finally demanding it all.

"Is not the land of Florida ours?" he demanded, hotly. "Have we not held it for hundreds of winters and summers? Then why should we go and come only at the nod of the paleface?"

"You talk like a fool," said Enematkla, who had come to a council of the Seminoles to urge the signing of this new treaty. "Three summers ago our fathers signed a treaty giving the white men the greater part of this country. Now they generously promise us much land in the West, over beyond the Father of Waters. Here we have only this reservation and part of it swampland—"

"Yes—and why?" interrupted Osceola. "It was because our fathers foolishly gave up the rest of our land of Florida. And what did we get for it? Nothing. Within nine years—as the white man counts time—we are driven out even from that. And who knows that the Americans will keep their word in this second treaty, or that the lands in the far West will be as good as they say?"

Enematkla shrugged his shoulders. "We must go, or fight," he answered. "The white men have more men and more guns. They are like the sands of the sea."

"And we"—retorted Osceola—"are like the lapping tide which can eat away the sands of the sea. This is my home. If the white man wants me to go somewhere else, he can come and get me!"

The younger warriors grunted approval at this. Osceola was still only one of the rank and file, but here was a man worth listening to. As his words were carried to other towns and camps in the peninsula, they fell upon eager ears and soon messengers came seeking him for their councils. He went, he argued, he pleaded with them to fight to save their homes, and to this appeal—as old as the dawn of time—they harkened.

"We will fight if you will lead us," they answered.

And thus it was that Osceola became leader of the Seminoles.

As he stood glancing around at his company of picked warriors, he looked every inch a chief. Tall, slender, but finely proportioned, he reminded one of a vigorous young sapling which will bend but not break before the hurricane. His clean-cut features were pleasant, though he had a somewhat sad expression, like Lincoln. His skin, lighter than that of most Indians, revealed his Caucasian strain. His eyes were large and expressive and could flash fire upon occasion. His mind was keen and alert, and although he was not a chief by descent the other warriors instinctively followed his counsel.

How able it was is shown by the stern records of history. For seven years he successfully resisted the American forces, and it cost the lives of fifteen hundred white soldiers and the expenditure of ten millions of dollars to bring his war to a close—and then only by an act of treachery on the part of the white men—but we are anticipating our story.

The first move on the part of Osceola was to convey the non-combatants—the old men, the women, and the children—down into the central part of Florida—into the heart of the Everglades where it would be hard to follow them. Florida, as we know, has thousands of acres of low-lying land, filled with bogs and overgrown with live oaks, cypresses, and other thick growth. Here and there in the Everglades, as they are called, are higher hummocks of earth, sometimes several acres in extent, of dry, arable land. The Indians through centuries had learned every secret trail to these hidden spots, and here they could dwell in comparative security.

The task confronting the American soldiers was formidable in the extreme—as they soon learned. Osceola proved a veritable swamp fox, doubling on his tracks, here to-day and gone to-morrow. To his banner rallied nearly all the scattered clans of the Seminoles and also hundreds of Negroes, escaped slaves who had taken refuge in the interior and intermarried with the Indians.

The spark which set off the conflagration was caused by a private wrong. Osceola's wife, Ouskaloosa, it was claimed, had Negro blood in her veins. One day while affairs were outwardly at peace, he went with her on a visit to Fort King. The officer in charge looked questioningly at the attractive young squaw.

"She is the daughter of a slave; she belongs to us," he said, and ordered his men to take her into custody.

The terrified Ouskaloosa uttered a scream and rushed into her husband's arms for protection,— only to be roughly torn from him. Osceola was powerless to prevent this outrage, but as he stalked forth from the fort he inwardly vowed his whole life to vengeance.

Weeks went by, and as reports filtered into the fort of the unrest among the Seminoles the soldiers kept under cover, while they awaited reinforcements. Three days after Christmas, in 1835, the first blow of reprisal was struck. General Thompson was waylaid outside his post with half a dozen of his men. While going along a narrow shaded path, he heard a shot ring out followed by a war-whoop. The trunks of the trees round about seemed suddenly to become alive with painted warriors. Taken completely by surprise the officer and his handful of men could make but feeble resistance. They were slain and scalped—and soon the news was sent by fast relays to the North, that the Second Seminole War was on.

In the guerrilla fighting which ensued, first one side and then the other was victorious. Osceola would not risk a general engagement; his plan was to strike at unexpected points—a plan which the nature of the terrain made possible. As one after another army officer was sent against him, he would skilfully elude him until it suited Osceola's purpose to make a stand.

One engagement sent a thrill of horror through the nation at the north; but was celebrated at Indian campfires flickering through the Everglades and lighting up the painted bodies of dancing warriors, many of whom held aloft gory scalplocks taken from their enemies. Major F. L. Dade had been sent to one of Osceola's reputed strongholds, to ferret him out. His company consisted of a hundred men, with a few Indian scouts. The white men were picked soldiers and trained woodsmen, but as they made their painful way through the dense woods and across the treacherous bogs, they realized that Nature herself was fighting with the Indians and against them. Here and there open bits of water would show themselves, and sluggish streams. What seemed to be a half-sunken log would disappear from sight with a dull splash. It was an alligator. Snakes wriggled their sinuous way across their path; and here, there, and everywhere were mosquitoes.

Save for these and the usual sounds of the march all was quiet and peaceful. The enemy had not shown himself, and presumably the swamp fox was only making his way to another lair. Such may have been Major Dade's thoughts, but he never relaxed his vigilance for a minute. The very Everglades themselves seemed full of menace. He shook off the feeling of foreboding which persisted, and ordered his men to advance. It was impossible for them to keep together on the trail. They strung out often in single file as they made their way along. Finally they came to a more open space bordered with a thicket on the farther side. As they emerged into the clearing, the air suddenly became full of whizzing arrows, with the occasional dull drone of a bullet. Osceola had turned upon them and attacked.

"Stand and fire, men!" ordered the Major, sharply, at the same time drawing his sword and springing forward.

These were his last words, for as he advanced a tall, sinuous Indian sprang to meet him. The brave wielded a long spear, which he hurled with terrific force. The weapon transfixed the officer's breast and he fell mortally wounded. At the same moment, the war-cry of Osceola rang out—a long-drawn-out wail like the howl of a wolf. His men responded with yelps like the shrill barking of dogs. Fiercely they fought— not like other Indians who struck and then fell back, but standing their ground resolutely. They had the twofold advantage of surprise and numbers. The little clearing within a few moments resembled a shambles. One by one the soldiers went down, fighting to the last, until of the hundred only one man was left alive.

In the white man's annals, only the defense of the Alamo and Custer's last fight—both of a later day—can be compared with this massacre.

When the news came back to the States, there was widespread grief, a fierce denunciation of the War Department, and above all else a general clamor: "Take Osceola, dead or alive!" To the white people he was not a patriot seeking to protect his homeland from the invader; he was only an Indian who must be destroyed by fair means or foul.

General Jessup was despatched to the seat of conflict, with urgent instructions to seize and hold this trouble-maker. He finally accomplished his task, but in no way creditable to the white race. The general, on his arrival in Florida, invited the Indians to a parley, in which all their grievances were to be ironed out and a new treaty made. He sent Cherokee runners to seek out the headquarters of Osceola, bearing this message of peace. After some days of searching, they finally reached him. Osceola listened to the message gravely.

"The white general talks smoothly," he said, after they had ended; "but I have long since found that the white man speaks with a double tongue. How can I trust him, even in an open parley?"

"The general bids you come to him under a flag of truce," was the answer. "The white flag is the emblem of peace, and as such is universally respected."

Long Osceola and his braves debated the matter. Should they put themselves within the power of the white man even under a flag of truce; or should they fight it out in their own way? At last the words of the messengers prevailed, and they resolved to meet their foe in a powwow. Following the lead of the Cherokee scouts Osceola and eighty of his men went to General Jessup's camp, which was near St. Augustine. In front of them floated the white flag of truce—the one flag that, it was said, all men respected.

As they neared the garrison, the general and his staff rose to meet them, while a file of soldiers far outnumbering the braves stood on either side. Osceola saw the cordon of his enemies, but his eyes did not flinch; he only glanced at them with proud disdain.

"My white father has sent for me," he said, when he had come within hearing of the general, "and I am here."

"Welcome, Osceola," replied the general; "let us talk and be friends, instead of fighting."

"What does my white father have to offer his children?" countered Osceola.

In the parley which followed, the terms of the old treaty were rehearsed and insisted upon. The Seminoles were to lay down their arms and submit to the Americans. They must forsake their homes and go across the Mississippi.

Osceola smiled scornfully. "There is nothing new in this," he answered. "Why call me from my home to tell me old men's talk?" And he was obdurate.

As the general offered final arguments as to why it was to the Indians' best interests to surrender and go peaceably, rather than be hunted down like wild beasts, Osceola only replied:

"I will die first. Now Osceola and his warriors must depart."

As he turned to go, the general lifted his hand. It was a preconcerted signal, and instantly the white soldiers closed in on the Seminoles from all sides. The Indians' weapons had previously been laid on the ground beneath a large oak, and Osceola saw at a glance that he was trapped.

The young chieftain at first looked with amazement at the soldiers who surrounded him. Then as he realized the depth of the treachery, his expressive eyes flashed contempt and anger.

"So this is your vaunted white flag of truce, and the honor of the white people?" he taunted.

Later when the officers would parley with him
further, offering him his freedom upon certain
conditions, he remained stonily silent. He was
like an eagle taken captive by a snare, but with
proud spirit unbroken. Even when conveyed to
Fort Moultrie, S. C., and kept in a dark dungeon, he would not yield. He refused to eat and
died unconquered. This was in the year 1838,
and now, nearly a century later, his dungeon is
still pointed out to curious sightseers, and his
grave guarded by an iron fence is still here—one
of the few civilian graves ever dug on Government soil.

When the news was sent by swift horsemen to
the North, that Osceola was taken, at first there
was great popular rejoicing. But when the de-
tails of his capture were learned, the same public
which had urged on the War Department now
censured it for the action. Great sympathy was
shown for his fate. Had the prisoner of war
known of this shame on the part of the white
race, his cup of bitterness might not have been
quite so full.

As for the other Seminoles, one after another
their strongholds were captured, and their
families made prisoners. In August, 1842,
the remnant sued for peace, and were given the
same terms which Osceola had scornfully re-
jected—the absolute removal of the tribe from

Florida. They had perforce to submit, and sorrowfully took their places, with their families, on board the long file of army wagons headed west. They were sent to Oklahoma where, it is pleasant to note, they were given good ground and soon began to prosper. They took on a fair amount of civilization, and were known as one of the "Five Civilized Tribes." Their tribal government, however, came to an end in 1906, when their lands were opened to white settlement. At that time there were about three thousand in all, only one-third being of pure Seminole blood; the rest were partly Negro.

It is of final interest to note that a remnant of the tribe never left Florida. They succeeded in eluding the authorities and sticking to their old haunts in the Everglades. They were classed as outlaws, and the government paid little attention to them except to see that they did not do any damage to their neighbors. There were only three or four hundred of these at the last counting—a pathetic remnant of what was once a powerful people.

CHAPTER TWELVE

"HE will be a great chief; he has already brought in his first scalp!"

Thus proudly spoke one squaw to another, pointing to a lad of fifteen, well grown for his age, who was returning to the village with a victorious party of his elders. The squaw was his mother, and her praise was natural. The taking of the first scalp of an enemy was a signal event.

The young man himself tried to look unconcerned as he saw the glances of the women and the maidens upon him. It behooved a brave to be superior to flattery, as well as to suffering, but he could not forbear to strut a little. He had grown up overnight. He was no longer a boy; he was a brave, with a scalp dangling at his belt. Hereafter he could go on all the war-trails, and take part in all the councils.

Black Hawk—which is the English for a long Indian name meaning the same thing—was the son of one of the lesser chiefs of the Sacs, or Sauk tribe, living out in the western part of Illinois

237

near the mouth of Rock River. Their allies were the Fox Indians, and together they went on their forays which made the joint name of Sacs and Foxes a terror for many years, but chiefly among other tribes. Black Hawk had been reared in this atmosphere of hostility, and it was therefore natural for him to think of war as the only means to establish one's own prowess. He had practised archery and the throwing of the tomahawk from the time he was big enough to walk; and when the white man's weapon with its leaden bullet became familiar to his people, he lost no time in learning its secret also. And so it is not surprising that we behold him, a youth of fifteen, coming home with his first bloody trophy, taken from an Indian foe.

Two years later his tribe went again on the warpath, this time against the Osages, who had been invading the lands of the Sacs and Foxes, and had set up a fortified village in the center of their hunting grounds. Black Hawk went eagerly with others on a surprise attack which routed the enemy; and again he returned with a dripping scalp at his girdle. The older braves began to speak of him, as he hoped they would, for he had an overmastering ambition. Though only the son of a lesser chief, he aspired to be the head chief of the two tribes.

Eager for more scalps, he persuaded his fel-

lows to attack another Osage camp, but after a
forced march they found it deserted. The other
braves, not caring to go back empty-handed and
face the ridicule of the village, began to blame
him for this fool's errand.

"Go on home," he retorted, scornfully. "Black
Hawk does not return without a scalp."

Nor did he. Leaving them, he plunged alone
into the forest, and a few days later arrived at
the village with two more of these trophies at his
belt; but not a word would he utter as to his
adventures.

For such deeds as this he became, when only
nineteen, the acknowledged leader of the warlike
part of the two tribes. He led a company of
two hundred against the Osages, with the purpose of annihilating them or driving them out
of the country. But the Osages mustered an
army of equal strength, and the battle which resulted was desperate and bloody. It did not
settle anything. Black Hawk, however, increased his reputation as a scalp-taker, for he
slew five braves with his own hand.

His next expedition was not so fortunate.
This time it was against the Cherokees. It was
a surprise attack and successful in that no less
than twenty-eight of the enemy were slain, and
only seven of his people. One of the seven, however, was his father, and great was the sorrowing

in camp when the loss was known. Black Hawk's warlike ambitions received a severe setback. He saw that a great chief must have other qualities than a mere ability to "lift hair." He also saw that some of the other chiefs, such as Keokuk, kept a great influence over the tribe by their ability to speak in council. He took this lesson so much to heart, that for five years he refrained from warfare, studying instead the ways of the medicine men and prophets. He tried to acquire fame as a man of supernatural power. Nevertheless, he never forgave the Cherokees for his father's death—although in battle—and when next his tribe went against them, he was in the forefront. Again they found the enemy's village almost deserted. Only four men and a woman were left.

"These prisoners are mine," he said; and the others respecting his superior rights to revenge did not object.

The four Cherokee braves looked him in the face, expecting nothing less than death, but the older Black Hawk was not quite so bloodthirsty as the boy had been.

"Go," he said, cutting their bonds. "You are too few in number for Black Hawk to glut his revenge." The amazed men were set free, while the woman was taken back to his own camp.

Black Hawk's name began to be heard and

feared among the white settlers during the War of 1812 between the United States and England. The latter had succeeded in forming alliances with most of the tribes along the Illinois and Mississippi, among them the Sacs and Foxes. But Black Hawk disdained ways of peace. It was a turbulent time indeed for the dwellers along the borders. There were few American soldiers to protect the outposts, while the British from their Canadian frontier could and did give the Indians ammunition and other supplies. Black Hawk had a picked body of men which dashed from one frontier town to another striking a sudden blow and then vanishing. His name became one of terror. Fortunate indeed it was that this war between England and America was of short duration. With the dawn of peace sturdy riflemen poured in from Kentucky, Virginia, and Ohio, and the Indians again had to retreat to the west.

This steady retreat before the arms of the paleface rankled in the soul of Black Hawk. He saw the whole of the land east of the Mississippi being taken by them. His own people living on the great river were almost the last. And now agents from the hated government at Washington were treating with them to take away their lands also, giving them other tracts still farther toward the setting sun. He bitterly reproached

Chief Keokuk in council for furthering this treaty.

Keokuk had been his lifelong rival; he hated the very sight of him. Keokuk was a smooth talker, he said, who stayed at home when others went on the warpath, and made treaties with their enemies. Black Hawk envied him his powers of persuasion and influence, and had tried to emulate them in the five years when he laid aside the tomahawk. Keokuk himself was not a chief by birth, but rose to a place of importance through his marked ability and force of character. It was said that his mother was half French. At an early age he had been admitted to the councils of the Sacs, not through scalp-taking, but because they said he had a long head on his shoulders. While Black Hawk and his party were constantly out stirring up trouble with the neighboring tribes, it was Keokuk's policy to cement as many alliances as possible—a much wiser plan in the long run, as the Indians could only hope to make a stand against the white men by sticking together.

The Sacs had a guest lodge, to which any visitor, white or Indian, was welcome, and his person was sacred while he was their guest. Keokuk was made the keeper of the lodge, and so genial was he, with such an inexhaustible fund of stories, both eloquent and humorous, that he became famous for miles around. His tribe was quick to see the value of this guest lodge, and they provided him with funds at the tribal expense to maintain it in a sumptuous manner. The wily Keokuk used it as a further means of widening his own influence over the tribes—and the man of war, Black Hawk, could only grind his teeth in impotent rage.

Twenty years went by. The War of 1812 had become but a memory. The great tract known as the Northwest Territory was being carved into the states of Ohio, Indiana, Illinois, Michigan, and Wisconsin. By the same token, the hunting lands of the Indians were disappearing. We have told in other chapters of the wars led by Pontiac, Tecumseh, Little Turtle, and others to regain it. Always the answer was the same. Black Hawk saw and pondered. Unless something were done and done quickly, not an Indian lodge would be left on the eastern bank of the Mississippi.

As early as 1804 the Americans under General Harrison had negotiated a treaty with the Sacs and Foxes, by which the Indians had ceded an immense tract of land lying between the Illinois and Mississippi rivers. For this they received goods to the value of two thousand dollars, with a further annuity of the same amount, and the promise of the protection of the United States against their foes. Keokuk had agreed to this treaty, but Black Hawk had raged against both the sale of lands and the "protection." He felt that it was belittling to receive such aid. One article in the treaty, however, provided that "the Indians belonging to the said tribes shall enjoy the privilege of living and hunting" on the land.

However, a clause such as this doesn't mean much when the land is being rapidly built upon. Illinois was made an independent state in 1818, and settlers poured into its fertile prairies in increasing numbers. Little if any attention was paid to the Indians' rights during this settlement. This was a "white man's country," and if the natives didn't like it, they could get out. More than one injustice was done the friendly Sacs and Foxes, in the covert hint to them that it was time for them to move along.

It is true—on the other side—that these two tribes violated their treaty of peace by siding with the British in the War of 1812; although a peaceable faction headed by Keokuk remained at home. After this war the old treaty was confirmed, in 1815, at a grand council held at Portage des Sioux. A small party, however, led by Black Hawk still held out. In an impassioned speech he protested against the cession of the tribal lands, and said that the treaty was made by only a portion of his tribe, and therefore was not binding. But the records show that all the leading chiefs of the Sacs and Foxes signed the treaty, and at this time he was not recognized as the head chief, despite his pretensions.

The proud spirit of Black Hawk suffered a further indignity, although it was largely of his own doing. The American government grew tired of the perpetual tribal disputes along the border, such as the turbulent Black Hawk loved, and tried to end them once for all. To this end, they held a big conclave at Prairie du Chien, in 1825, when the American commissioners, William Clarke and Lewis Cass, met the chiefs of the Sacs, Foxes, Winnebagoes, Sioux, Chippewas, and other tribes of the Northwest, and tried to pacify their disputes. Certain definite tracts of land were set aside for each tribe, and the others were forbidden to trespass thereon. Wide distances were to separate their boundaries, and it was thought that each tribe would thus not molest the others. But the white commissioners' plan failed to put an end to the hostilities. The ink was scarcely cold upon the treaty, when news began to sift in of petty outrages and attacks.

In one of these forays on the river, Red Bird, a Sioux chief, and Black Hawk were caught "red-handed." They were clapped into a military prison, which must have been torture indeed to their proud souls. It was like putting untamed eagles behind the bars. Red Bird, in fact, died there. Black Hawk was confined for more than a year. When finally brought to trial he was set free for want of legal evidence. At this his rage flared forth anew.

"If I was innocent, why did they keep me in bonds?" he demanded; and went his way vowing still further vengeance.

This took the form of an attempted confederation of all the tribes, from the Rock River clear down to the Mexican border, in one last stand against the white man. In his own account of this, which has come down to us, he says: "Runners were sent to the Arkansas, Red River, and Texas—not on the subject of our lands, but on a secret mission, which I am not permitted at present to explain." His gigantic plot, however, went by the boards. Black Hawk was a fighter, but lacked the executive ability of a Pontiac or a Tecumseh.

By the terms of the treaty of 1804, the Sacs and Foxes had been allowed to remain on their lands on the eastern side of the Mississippi, which they had held for many generations, but by their new treaty of 1830 they agreed to remove to the other side. The Iowas, the Sioux, and some other tribes were parties to this agreement, but again Black Hawk held out—partly against the white men and partly against the growing power of his old rival, Keokuk. He denounced the latter as having white blood in his veins and having sold his country for nothing, and proceeded to go again on the warpath. Organizing a band of a hundred or more braves, as restless and unruly as himself, he rode back into Illinois determined to hold his ancient lands to the last man. They were well mounted and all had modern guns, so it was a formidable uprising.

The chief village of the Sacs was on a point of land formed by the Rock River and the Mississippi. It was a fertile river bottom of about seven hundred acres, which had been planted in corn. To this day some of the finest corn in the United States is grown roundabout, some of the stalks reaching the height of ten or twelve feet. Squashes and other vegetables grew thriftily with very little labor on the part of the squaws, while just back of the little peninsula dense woods formed the natural habitat of abundant wild game. The rivers supplied fish generous in size and numbers. So it is small wonder that the Sacs did not want to relinquish their home of a century or more.

For some months, however, Black Hawk remained outwardly peaceful, until an incident made him boiling mad. When his men came back home in the spring of 1831, after their usual winter's hunt, they found white settlers in possession of their village. The braves perforce took possession of the lands adjoining, and their squaws began to clear the ground for the season's crops. The white men thereupon ordered the Indians off. They refused to go, and the governor was appealed to. He in turn wrote to General Gaines for military assistance to remove the Indians—"peaceably if they could; forcibly if they must." General Gaines rode toward the village with a small escort, only to be met by Black Hawk, who told him that the Indians would never give up the home of their fathers. Gaines wrote an official report to the Secretary of War, in which he said:

I have visited the Rock River villages, to ascertain the localities and dispositions of the Indians. They are resolved to abstain from hostilities, except in their own defence. Few of their warriors were to be seen. Their women, children, and old men appeared to be anxious, but none attempted to run off. I am resolved to abstain from firing a shot without some bloodshed, or some manifest attempt to shed blood on the part of the Indians. I have already induced nearly one-third of them to cross the Mississippi. The residue say they will not cross; and their women urge their husbands to fight rather than abandon their homes.

General Gaines at once recruited the militia and they marched against Black Hawk. He was not yet ready to fight, and retreated. The soldiers burned the Indian lodges and destroyed their farms. The general then sent scouts to demand that the Indians hold a peace council, on June 30. Black Hawk sullenly came with twenty-seven of his followers, and agreed to take their families across the Mississippi.

During the ensuing fall and winter, however, the rebel chieftain again tried to stir up many western tribes. He sent runners in every direction, despite the efforts of Keokuk to stop him, and so successful was he this time, that by the spring of 1832 he had again crossed the big river at the head of a throng estimated at two thousand, about five hundred of whom were warriors. General Gaines saw that he had a full-sized war on his hands. An alarm was immediately sounded throughout the border, and the dread words of former years, "the Indians are on the warpath," sent a shiver into the homes of many an isolated settler. They knew from the tales of their fathers what to expect when Indians went on the warpath seeking blood and scalps—and Black Hawk had been known all his life as a scalp-taker.

Regiments of militia were hastily mustered in, but they were poorly disciplined and equipped, and unused to Indian fighting. Two brigades under Isaiah Stillman were sent up the river toward the chief's headquarters. On the way

they were met by three Indians bearing a flag
of truce. While they were parleying, the heads
of other Indians were seen peering from behind
some bushes. Fearing treachery, shots were fired
by the green soldiers and one of the flag-bearers
was shot down. Instantly a war-whoop resounded and the woods seemed alive with yelling,
painted natives. The settlers tried to make a
stand, but as usual in such surprise attacks they
were at a disadvantage. Panic seized them; they
threw away their weapons and a disgraceful rout
followed. Amid all the din the stentorian voice
of Black Hawk was heard: "Kill! kill!" For
thirty miles, it is said, the retreat was made. The
attack was at a small creek since known as "Stillman's Run," not from the swiftness of the current, but the flight.

This defeat created still further consternation
in the borders. While Governor Reynolds hastily
called for a citizen soldiery of three thousand "to
subdue the Indians and drive them out of the
state," Black Hawk unloosed his dogs of war.
On many a lonely house or isolated community
he suddenly darted—killing the men and carrying off the women and children. In one such settlement at Indian Creek, in La Salle County,
the white men tried to stand against him, but fifteen were killed and the houses burned to the
ground.

Two young girls by the name of Hall were captured at another place and forced to go with a band of a hundred men, on a forced march of four days. They were not mistreated, however, and were given food, although their hands were tied. Reaching an Indian camp they were turned over to some squaws, who gave them to understand that they were to be the brides of two braves then on the warpath. Their faces were streaked with red, blue and black, while men, women, and children danced around them— doubtless adopting them into the tribe. They were then given a feast of fried venison, corncakes, and fried leeks.

Fortunately for them, on their next journey— for the Indians did not stay long in one place— they met a Frenchman who befriended them and persuaded the Indians to agree to their ransom. He conducted them to a Winnebago village, where the terms of ransom were agreed upon, and the girls were taken back to a fort at White Oak Springs. There what was their joy to meet an older brother, who had been at work in the fields and thus escaped the massacre.

Many such tales not so happy in their ending began to be heard throughout the countryside— some of them exaggerated no doubt, but none the less fearsome in the telling. But the settlers after the first shock of surprise were no cowards.

They set to work grimly with the object of meeting and defeating Black Hawk. Easier said than done. He was as elusive as the bird for which he was named. Throughout his series of forays and skirmishes, which were in the nature of guerrilla raids, he was seldom seen, and only small bodies of his men were encountered.

On the 24th of June he did make one surprise attack upon Apple River Fort, but was repulsed. When a battalion headed by Major Dement endeavored to drive him out, he turned fiercely and hurled his men at the soldiers' throats. For several hours this small but savage battle lasted, ending with victory for the Indians, but at a heavy loss. Black Hawk was not overjoyed as he looked over the field that night. He knew that a few more such victories would wipe out his forces.

His worst fears were realized soon after. Hearing through his scouts that a still larger army was on his trail, headed by General Henry, he retreated to White Water, Wisconsin, and there tried to make a stand. But the general by a forced march of four days came up with him, and prevented him from crossing the river. The two armies came together at sundown and, tired as it was, the white one charged. They knew that overnight the Indians would either elude them or make a surprise attack. Black Hawk's men were in a little ravine near the Wisconsin. They were first discovered when an advance company of whites was fired upon. Immediately the sound of firing filled the air, amid the yells of the Indians, while the remainder of the attacking army came on at full speed.

General Henry with the skill of a campaigner quickly formed his army into a hollow square, with men facing in every direction. Black Hawk tried to crumple up one side but failed. A flank attack on two other sides also ended in failure. His men were met with shots, no matter from what quarter they showed themselves. In the dying light of day the scene resembled an inferno of struggling men. No quarter was asked or given. After an Indian had discharged his gun he dashed madly into close conflict with knife or tomahawk. With nightfall, however, the firing ceased and the cries of the Indians indicated that they were in full retreat.

The weary white army made no move to follow them. Posting strong pickets they lay down and slept almost in their tracks. The next morning's sun revealed a frightful carnage. Sixty-eight warriors had been killed outright; others were dying; and still others had doubtless been carried off by their comrades. The American loss was slight, thanks to their close formation.

Black Hawk himself succeeded in getting

across the river, with a still formidable remnant of his men; but the Americans were now in close pursuit. On the 2nd of August they came up with him again, at the mouth of the Bad Axe River, and another desperate struggle ensued. Black Hawk was indeed a fighter, and now he realized that his back was to the wall. The wall in this case was the river itself, and in the fierce stand before the onrushing Americans under General Atkinson, one hundred and fifty of his men were slain or driven into the current; while forty more were captured. It was in vain for him to sing his death-chant of "Kill! kill!" His star had set. Seeing his men scattered and defeated, he mounted his swift pony and fled to the north—an exile from the land of his fathers with a price set upon his head.

Thus ended the Black Hawk War—a brief but sanguinary and perilous time. It had turned the whole frontier state of Illinois into an armed camp. So swift was the march of events, however, that hundreds of recruits, who had been drilling and marching, never saw an Indian. One such recruit, a lank country lawyer of Springfield, standing six feet six in his stocking feet, told many humorous stories of his own experiences. He was a humorous fellow anyhow, and used to convulse his audience whenever he got upon the topic of the Black Hawk War.

"Why," he would say, with his famous, nasal drawl, "I never did see any live, fighting Indians. But I did have a good many bloody struggles with the mosquitoes!"

And he would go on to relate about how his horse was stolen from him, miles from nowhere up in Michigan, and how he had struggled back about two hundred miles on foot or by canoe through almost impassable country.

"Learned a lot about the country and about the roads that we didn't have," he would conclude; "but never had a chance to come to grips with that fellow, Black Hawk—no *sir!*"

The lank countryman who was thus tasting his first and only actual service became later known to fame as Abraham Lincoln.

As for Black Hawk, his cup of bitterness was full. Taken prisoner by the Winnebagoes and delivered by them to the Americans, he was held a close prisoner. Then he heard that his rival, Keokuk, had through his efforts for peace been elevated to the supreme chieftaincy of the tribe. The prisoner gnashed his teeth in impotent rage. A few days later the two leaders confronted each other at a parley with the white men. They formed a striking contrast. Keokuk was dignified but temperate and quiet in his speech—a diplomat who had won far more for his tribe than his turbulent brother. Black Hawk, every inch a warrior, still shot forth glances of fire from his darting black eyes—like the hawk that he was. Well-named, he struck first and reasoned afterwards. At last, losing all control over his emotions, he strode across the council ring to where Keokuk sat.

"Coward! Seller of my country!" he exclaimed; and whipping off his clout he struck Keokuk across the face with it.

Instantly the council was in an uproar. It was a deadly insult. But braves and soldiers jumped between them. Keokuk, who had sprung to his feet, only drew his blanket tightly about his shoulders and looked scornfully at his rival.

"Black Hawk behaves like a child," he said. "He could always reason better with his fists than with his head."

In order to avoid further trouble, the military authorities decided to take Black Hawk to an eastern prison. He made no protest other than to utter an impassioned speech of farewell to his tribe, in which he said:

My warriors have fallen around me. I see my evil day at hand. The sun rose clear on us in the morning, and at night it sank in a dark cloud and looked like a ball of fire. This was the last sun that shone on Black Hawk. He is now a prisoner to the white man; but he can stand torture; he is not afraid of death; he is no coward. Black Hawk is an Indian; he has done nothing of which an Indian need to be ashamed. He has fought the battles of his country against the white men who came year after year to cheat them, and take away their lands. You know the cause of our making war—it is known to all white men—they ought to be ashamed of it. The white men despise the Indians and drive them from their homes. The white men do not scalp the head, but they do worse—they poison the heart. Black Hawk is satisfied. He will go to the world of spirits contented. Farewell to my nation! Farewell to Black Hawk!

It is not surprising that a warrior with this indomitable spirit should prove of great interest to the white men. He was taken to Fortress Monroe, Virginia, but confined there only a month—striking up a great friendship with the commander. Then he was taken, still as a prisoner of war, on a tour of the principal cities, where he made speeches on behalf of the Indians, and was given close attention. On his return west it is interesting to note that he made a truce with Keokuk, and even went with the latter on a special trip to Washington. He heard Keokuk make an eloquent plea before the authorities there, in debate with the Sioux and other tribes respecting boundary lines. As a result of this speech the claim of the Sacs and Foxes was held valid. It greatly increased the prestige of Keokuk, and even Black Hawk had to nod his head in approval and say, "Good medicine!" Had he united in his own person the wisdom and eloquence of Keokuk, with his own bravery and skill in battle, the white men would have had a foe indeed.

Keokuk died in 1848, in Kansas, whither he had migrated; but in 1883 his remains were brought back to the banks of the Mississippi, and there buried by the white men, under a monument showing his effigy looking east over the great river toward the home of his fathers. It stands on a bluff in a park in the thriving western city which bears his name—Keokuk, Iowa.

As for Black Hawk, he was released on parole and never again took up arms against the Americans. After his trip east with Keokuk he settled on the Des Moines River, where he met a peaceful end, October 3, 1838. He was given an imposing funeral, such as his vainglorious soul must have loved. His body was dressed in a uniform presented by General Andrew Jackson, with a sword from the same donor. In the other hand was a cane given him by Henry Clay. In life he had met defeat; but in death he was honored even by his enemies.

CHAPTER THIRTEEN

A HUNDRED years ago there roamed the plains of the West one of the most powerful of all Indian confederations. Only the Algonquins in the East equalled them in point of numbers. From the Mexican border roaming on both sides of the Mississippi River, east at times as far as the Carolinas, and west as far as the Rockies, the scattered tribes, although speaking different dialects, had the same racial characteristics, and were among the most warlike of all the Indians. What they saw they took, and woe betide the foeman who stood in the way. By some they were called the Dakotas; by others, the Sioux, which is from a Chippewa name meaning "snake" or "adder"—hence, in the picturesque Indian speech, an "enemy."

Gradually the Sioux moved northward to the headwaters of the Mississippi and the Missouri, and after many clashes with white men and Indians alike, they sat sullenly back upon their haunches prepared to hold this chosen land against all comers. When the scouts at their council fires reported the growing numbers and aggressions of the paleface, the medicine men grunted savagely. Let the weak-kneed Indians of the East flee before this usurper; when he came into the Sioux country there would be a different story to tell!

One of the great Sioux medicine men of a century ago was Sitting Bull, the elder. He was both medicine man and chief, a mighty hunter and fighter. For his prowess in chasing the buffalo, he had been christened "Sitting Buffalo Bull," but this had been shortened to Sitting Bull. His chief hunting lodge was on the Grand River, in South Dakota, and here, in the year 1834 a son was born to him, who was called Jumping Badger, as he learned to run and jump almost before he could walk. At the age of ten he could outstrip even the jackrabbit, and he brought in many a bit of small game just by running it to earth.

This fleetness of foot brought him further notice from the tribe when, at the age of fourteen, he accompanied his father on the warpath against the Crows. In the fracas an arrow struck a distant Crow warrior in the breast and he fell from his pony. With exultant whoops the Sioux braves charged in to retrieve the scalp. But a stripling was ahead of them. Dashing at full speed on foot, Jumping Badger arrived at the fallen enemy first, and was holding up the gory trophy when the older braves reached the spot. While he had not slain his man, he had secured his first scalp, without which no Indian lad could hope to become a first-class warrior.

The eye of his father gleamed with pride, and that night he made a great feast in the camp. Driving up a string of ponies from his private corral, he bade the braves to take their pick of them for their own use. Then placing his hand upon the shoulder of his son, he announced:

"Jumping Badger has come of age this day; he is no longer a lad, but a warrior. He shall be known no longer as Jumping Badger, the boy who hunts small game, but he shall bear my own name, Sitting Bull. He shall hunt big game, even men. I have spoken."

The other warriors gave a great shout at this, and thus it was that the younger Sitting Bull— the subject of this story—came into the councils of the tribe.

Were this a fanciful story, I should go on to tell of his deeds of bravery against the foe, and picture him in the glowing colors of a typical hero. But Sitting Bull does not come down to history in exactly this light. He was not a natural-born fighter, eager to go upon the war-path. Instead, he was a man of guile, winning

through craft what others sought to take with
their bare hands. His fleetness of foot even
earned for him the title of coward, but he was
only living out in his own life the adage:

> He who fights and runs away
> Shall live to fight another day.

However, at the council fire no tongue was
more crafty or more persuasive than his; no head
longer in planning. So he gained prestige rather
as a maker of medicine (the Indian name for
plans and plots) than as a warrior. He was
spoken of, by the Government agents, as crafty,
tricky, and a ready liar—but he himself felt that
deceit was part of the game! If he could pull
the wool over the eyes of the Inspectors, why, so
much the better. And even they gave him grudg-
ing praise. While they did not credit him with
any of the nobler qualities of the Indian,
no chief was more influential than he, and he
maintained his prestige until the day of his death.
"His medicine was good down to the end," said
one agent—and I imagine that old Sitting Bull
would not himself have wanted a better epitaph
than this.

As Sitting Bull grew to mature manhood, he
and the other chiefs saw their worst fears realized. The swelling tide of settlers was now
pouring across the Great River; their hunters

were making tremendous inroads upon the buffalo and other game; military posts were being set up; and the weaker tribes were being shunted farther and farther to the west. It was the period just before the Civil War of the white men, and an era of great "national expansion," in their parlance. But it spelled the doom of the Indians.

Sitting Bull was not blind. He watched every move of the hated intruder. He exhorted his followers to contest every inch of ground. By the time he had reached the age of thirty his name was known far and wide upon the Plains, as a sort of second Prophet. Often in those days he was seen on the warpath, and the settlers came to know him and fear him when, in 1866, he made a memorable raid upon Fort Buford. Indeed, during the sixties and seventies he was almost continually making war—either upon the Crows or Shoshonies, varied with sudden dashes upon the frontier posts. So he could not have been quite the "coward" some of the inspectors thought him to be.

The most influential chief of the Sioux, at this time, was Red Cloud—spoken of by various writers as one of the ablest Indians who ever lived. He sought to stem the tide of white invasion by diplomacy and treaty-making—much to the disgust of Sitting Bull and others of the

younger chiefs. Red Cloud it was who entered
into a treaty, in 1868, with an American commis-
sion headed by General William T. Sherman, of
Civil War fame. By this treaty the Sioux were
given the exclusive use of a reservation in the
Black Hills of South Dakota, which was bounded
by the Yellowstone River on the north; the Missouri on the east; the North Platte on the south;
and the Big Horn Mountains on the west. It
was one of the finest hunting preserves on the
continent. There roamed the buffalo, the elk,
the deer, the antelope, the bighorn sheep, the
grizzly bear, and myriads of smaller fur-bearing
animals. The rivers teemed with fish; the trees
with birds. Surely the Indian could not ask for
more than this.

But the wily Sitting Bull was not to be de-
ceived. He saw advancing hordes of white hunters on the Plains, killing off the bison by the
thousands—slaying them systematically for their
pelts alone, leaving their carcases to rot and their
bones to whiten where they fell. The Indians
had taken only enough each year for food and
raiment; the white man made a business of killing. The tragedy of the buffalo was the tragedy
of the Indian himself—and Sitting Bull knew it.
It required only a few short years to prove the
depth of this tragedy. General Sherman himself, in 1868, referred to this land as the "pasture-

fields of millions of buffalo, elk, deer, antelope, and other game"; but, only ten years later, stated: "Having traversed the Plains ten or fifteen times since that date, I can bear personal testimony that where, in 1868, millions of buffalo could be found, not a single one is now seen."

Another grievance of the Indians was the setting up of military posts within their territory. This had resulted in bloodshed prior to the treaty of 1868. Two years before this time, Fort Phil Kearney and Fort F. C. Smith had been established, despite the bitter protests of Red Cloud and his warriors. He demanded that they be dismantled, before any treaty-making was entered into. When the United States officers declined, he drew himself up haughtily and placing his hand upon his rifle declared: "In this and the Great Spirit I trust for the right!"

The short and savage war which resulted was his further answer. It has come down to history as "the tragedy of Fort Kearney." As this fort neared completion, the standing timber near at hand was exhausted. A group of woodsmen guarded by soldiers thereupon went into the forest to secure more lumber. Suddenly the air was rent with the warwhoop of Indians. It was a band of young braves under the leadership of Crazy Horse, a brilliant chief who later was heard from in larger battles. Instantly the soldiers answered shot with shot. The sounds of the conflict reached the distant walls of the fort, and reinforcements were hurriedly sent out. But the Indians did not retreat—the Sioux were not built that way; they pressed forward to a new attack, with shrill whoops. For an hour or more the fight raged, and only ended when the last white man had yielded up his life. The entire garrison of eighty-one had been wiped out to a man. It was a foretaste of the grim fate which awaited Custer, a few years later.

The American government saw that it must keep strict faith with the Sioux, in this matter of military posts, for Red Cloud, emboldened by his victory, "sat tight" and refused to sign any treaty until the last soldier and post had been removed from his land. This was finally done, and then only would he make peace. While it was a diplomatic victory for him, he lost prestige among his own people. The younger chiefs headed by Sitting Bull, Crazy Horse, Gall, and Black Moon, were bitter at the thought of making any terms whatever with the hated white man. In the active fighting which again broke out, after a few months, it was they who led the painted, shrieking warriors into battle. His sun had set.

The immediate cause of the renewal of hostilities was a military order signed by General

Phil. Sheridan, which when posted up and explained to the Sioux made them fighting mad. It read as follows:

All Indians when on their proper reservations are under the exclusive control and jurisdiction of their agents; . . . outside the well-defined limits of the reservation they are under the original and exclusive jurisdiction of the military authority; and as a rule will be considered hostile.

In other words, the proud Sioux could no longer come and go as they pleased; they had become the vassals of the paleface. Sitting Bull was at white heat.

"The Great Spirit made me," he cried; "and he did not make me an agency Indian!"

As a matter of cold fact, the government did not adhere to its treaty obligations in many essentials. It throughout regarded the Indians as an inferior race, to be exploited on every occasion when the rights of the two peoples conflicted. We have the word of General Sherman himself, on this point, when he said in an official report:

If the lands of the white man are taken, Civilization justifies him in resisting the invader. Civilization does more than this—it brands him as a coward and a slave if he submits to the wrong. Here Civilization made its own compact and guaranteed the rights of the weaker party. It did not stand by the guarantee. The treaty was broken, but not by the savage. If the savage resists, Civilization, with the Ten Commandments in one hand, and the sword in the other, demands immediate extermination.

In corroboration of this, let us quote from two others, who also knew conditions well. Said Major McLaughlin, an Indian Inspector:

The history of treaty making with the Sioux is the history of treaty making with all the Indians. The treaties were made for the accommodation of the whites, and broken when they interfered with the money-getters.

And this from General Sheridan, a few years later, which is the most melancholy of all:

There has been an insufficiency of food at the agencies, and as the game is gone, hunger has made the Indians in some cases desperate, and almost any race of men will fight rather than starve.

If the white leaders themselves made such statements in regard to their treaties, what must have been the sentiments of the braves in their councils! It was small wonder, indeed, that they viewed every fresh attempt at treaty-making with suspicion, and drew themselves aloof into their mountain fastnesses. During the fateful years leading up to the culminating tragedy of 1876, the government reports were full of rumors of unrest, and the name of Sitting Bull came

more and more into print. As restless braves left
the reservations to join his banner, by twos and
threes, and then scores, it was not long before
he had an army which caused the far-away
government at Washington much uneasiness.

While this war cloud was gathering momen-
tum, the government hit upon another astute
peace move. It invited the Sioux and other western tribes to send delegates to Washington, to
visit the "Great Father." The authorities reasoned that the Indians would be flattered by this
attention, and at the same time impressed by the
great resources of the white man's government
and the futility of trying to oppose it. So when
the visiting Indians reached the Capital, they
were received with an impressive parade of soldiery and taken with much pomp and circum-
stance to the White House.

Red Cloud, splendid in full regalia, headed a
group of fine-looking braves representing the
Oglala Sioux. Spotted Tail brought a company
of Brules. Other chiefs big and little stalked
in the procession which filed through the grounds
and portals of the White House, to shake
President Grant's hand.

But, at the same moment, away out in the
Black Hills, a stern-faced warrior called the roll
of the faithful. "The White Father strives to
steal our hearts away with flattery and bribes,"

he counselled; "stand firm!" And Black Moon, Crazy Horse, and Gall nodded their heads sagely, and said the same thing to their cohorts.

Hard upon the heels of this Washington conference, and as if in mockery of it, came reports and rumors of many petty outbreaks and outrages along the northwest border. Horses were stolen, crops were burned, no frontier cabin was safe; although little actual loss of life was reported. Whether or not Sitting Bull was directly responsible for all this, no one knows; but he was always blamed for it, and his name became a sort of bogey throughout the country. A scout who saw him at this time describes him as a warrior below medium height, but heavily and powerfully built, with chest unusually deep, shoulders broad, neck thick and short, and large head, with heavy-set jaws. His manner was quiet, and he had a certain proud air of superiority in dealing with all white men.

The Sioux, however, were by no means the only tribes that were giving trouble at this time. Out in Idaho the Piutes had been likewise unruly, and General Crook, a Civil War veteran and experienced plainsman, had been sent to subdue them. This he had accomplished successfully, and by way of reward he was next ordered into the Apache country. Here his campaign met with a similar outcome, and his name soon spread terror throughout the West. But when he was transferred to the Sioux country at the north, he met foemen worthy of his steel.

As a preliminary to his campaign, he sent Colonel Reynolds with six troops of cavalry to attack an Indian village. The month was March and the natives were still in winter quarters and therefore not expecting hostilities. By this surprise attack Crook sought to dishearten them and cause a general surrender. Marching all night in bitter cold weather, the cavalry came upon the village sheltered in a valley just before dawn. There were a hundred tepees in a compact group, and from their ridge-poles ascended curls of smoke. Each smoke plume represented a home, in which there were women and children.

It was a moment of peace and domesticity, broken the next by stark tragedy. Suddenly the shrill cry of an Indian scout told the soldiers that they were discovered, and warned the village of its danger. The scout paid for the warning with his life—as he expected—then down the slope and into the village swept the devastating troop. Soon the shrieks of women and children mingled with the hoarser shouts of men caught at death grapple. The Indians, taken by surprise, fled in every direction, and from the distant shelter of the woods saw their homes with all their stores demolished; the remnants of their families were exposed to the rigors of winter.

But Colonel Reynolds and his men made one mistake, that day. The village was the headquarters of Chief Crazy Horse, he of many battles and as implacable a foe of the white man as was Sitting Bull. It was like overturning a hornet's nest—as the soldiers presently discovered. Instead of taking to flight, Crazy Horse reformed his men and from the shelter of the trees began to take toll of the enemy. All day he hung on, retreating at one point only to strike again at another, until by nightfall Reynolds was in full retreat. The Indians, taken at disadvantage, and lacking the equipment and numbers of the whites, had yet proved their equals. Nor did they cease their harassing tactics after Reynolds had rejoined the main force under Crook. The entire army was forced back to its winter quarters at Fort Fetterman.

The failure of this expedition opened the eyes of the military authorities to the importance of the Sioux rebellion. Here was a formidable uprising of real fighting men, and under able generals. Accordingly a much larger force was sent out, known as the Yellowstone Expedition, and divided into three commands—one under General Crook, one under General Terry, and a third under General Custer, who, however, was attached to Terry's command.

In the latter part of May, Crook again started from Fort Fetterman, with the object of "cleaning up" the Indian country and making a junction with the other generals, if the Sioux still proved troublesome. On the 17th of June, while proceeding up the Rosebud River, in Montana, Crook once more met up with his old foe, Crazy Horse. Crook had at this time over a thousand soldiers, and some two hundred and sixty Shoshone and Crow scouts—a capable fighting force. But if he expected the Sioux to turn tail, he was again in for an unpleasant surprise. Far from retreating, the Indian army, which was about the size of his own, caught sight of their enemies with eager cries, and at once charged them. In a short but lively skirmish, the Indians once more had the better of it, and Crook retreated with a loss of ten killed and twice as many wounded. He deemed it the part of prudence to await reinforcements before hazarding a general battle.

The importance of this set-to, however, was great. The Indians were immensely heartened by this fresh victory; and Crook was prevented from joining Terry's forces, in the fateful battle of Little Big Horn, eight days later. As for Crazy Horse, he turned from this enemy and made haste to join the great army of Sioux gathering on the Little Big Horn.

Meanwhile, Terry, for some unaccountable reason, did not learn of the defeat of Crook, although his scouts had reported to him the movement of a large party of hostiles going up the Rosebud. They could tell this by the size of the trail. Terry at once detached Custer with his cavalry command, six hundred strong, and ordered him to follow the trail.

General George A. Custer was a fine-looking officer. He was a graduate of West Point and had served with distinction in the Northern army, attaining the rank of Major General. Later he had proved his mettle in fighting on the Plains. Out here he wore his hair long over his shoulders, Western style, to protect his neck from the heat, dust and insects. It was blond and curling, and gave him the sobriquet among the Indians of "Long Hair." A brave and gallant soldier was he, and an inspiring picture he and his troopers made, that June morning as they sounded "Boots and saddles" on the bugle and dashed out of camp, while their comrades waved them Godspeed. Little did those left behind realize that of all this gallant company not one would ever be seen again alive!

To Custer and his men it was just another job of catching up with fleeing Indians and putting

them to rout. It was all in the day's work. Six
hundred men well mounted should be ample; and
if not, the forces of both Terry and Crook were
not many miles away. Indeed, so confident were
they, that the cavalry was split into three parts—
one under Benteen to strike for the upper end
of an Indian encampment, which had been reported; a second under Reno, to head for the
Little Big Horn and engage the enemy when
found; while Custer, at the head of the "Fighting
Seventh," brought up the rear.

Meanwhile, had his scouts been taken aloft in
the airplanes of later days, what a sight would
have met their eyes. Up at the junction of the
Little Big Horn and Big Horn, in southeastern
Montana, the country was literally swarming
with Indians—Sioux, Cheyennes, and their allies.
And far from fleeing the enemy, they were ex-
ultantly awaiting his approach. Thousands there
were, decked in feathers, streaked with paint,
thirsting for the blood of their long-time enemy.
And down the valley only a few miles away rode
a thin line of men clad in buckskin and blue!

In the forefront of this powerful red army
were its most famous leaders—Gall, Crazy
Horse, Black Moon, Rain-in-the-Face, Big Man,
and others. Sitting Bull, while there, left the
actual command to these others; he was content
to pose as the Medicine Man—the one whose

potent spells would ensure victory. Runs-the-Enemy, a brave who later told of the incidents leading up to the fight, said: "Just at that time Sitting Bull made his appearance. He said, just as though I could hear him this moment, 'A bird, when it is on its nest, spreads its wings to cover the nest and eggs and protect them. It cannot use its wings for defense, but it can cackle and try to drive away the enemy. We are here to protect our wives and children, and we must not let the soldiers get them.' He was on a buckskin horse, and he rode from one end of the line to the other, calling out: 'Make a brave fight!'

"We were all hidden along the range of hills," this brave goes on to say. "While Sitting Bull was telling this, I looked up and saw that the Cheyennes had made a circle around Custer on the west, north, and east sides, and that left a gap on the south side for us to fill."

Since there was no white survivor of this unequal contest—for Custer soon found himself many times outnumbered, and his brave men could only take refuge behind their horses and continue to shoot until they were overwhelmed—the later stories of the Indians themselves are of unique interest. One of them, in telling of the fight, said: "Suddenly we heard firing, and we found that the soldiers were on us. The women and children were all frightened, and started to run across the hills, and we men mounted our horses and started toward the enemy." After describing how Reno's men were driven back, he continued: "We kept circling around Custer, and as his men came down the ridge we shot them down." Custer's men quickly dismounted and knelt behind their horses, and the braves kept circling round and round, but not coming to close quarters. By and by, the answering shots became fewer and finally ceased. The last soldier was killed.

"I did not see Custer fall," continued this brave, "for we did not know which one he was, and the white soldiers were all so mixed up that you couldn't tell one man from another."

The fighting, he said, lasted from daylight until three in the afternoon, and all the white men were killed. And that, reduced to its simplest terms, is the story of Custer's last stand. Like the defenders of the Alamo, not one lived to tell the tale. Two hundred and twelve of the flower of the Seventh Regiment of cavalry lay in ghastly heaps on the bloodstained ground. Fifty more were killed elsewhere, but Reno with part of his men escaped. Of the Indian loss, no one knows.

As for Sitting Bull, he had once again proved that his medicine was potent. His men had won a signal victory, as he had foretold, and though he himself had not struck a blow, he came out with far greater prestige than other chiefs.

Complete though the victory had been over Custer and Reno, the Indian leaders knew that it was not the part of wisdom to tarry here. After a night given over to feasting and rejoicing, and a day to dividing the spoils, this host of warriors melted away as quickly as it had gathered. When the rescuing armies of Terry and Crook reached the spot, only the heap of slain bore mute evidence, on that bloody slope, of the terrific conflict that had been waged to the death. Not a hostile Indian was to be seen.

As for Sitting Bull, he had pushed north with a force estimated at two thousand men, and did not pause until he had crossed the border into Canada. Here he knew he would be safe from pursuit and could treat with the enemy at his leisure. Not content with this, however, he endeavored to enlist the Blackfeet on his side. He sent a messenger to them with a piece of tobacco, which they were to smoke in token of their willingness to go with him back across the border.

"Come with us," said his spokesman. "We have destroyed the white man's forts; we have defeated him in pitched battle; we will drive him clear out of the Indian's land forever."

But Crowfoot, the head chief of the Blackfeet, regarded him sternly.

"No," he said. "We cannot smoke your tobacco on such terms; the whites are our friends, and we will not fight against them."

When this message was reported to Sitting Bull, he flushed with anger. "Go back and tell Crowfoot that we will go over the border without him," he said. "Then after we have defeated the whites, we will come back and take his lands and horses and women away from him."

Idle boast; for even then commissioners were being sent by both Canada and the United States to tell him to lay down his arms. They found him still full of fight, still the relentless foe of the whites. They were interlopers, he said, taking away the land that the Great Spirit had given to the Indians. Before his impassioned speeches, even the commissioners bowed with respect. To their requests for him to go back to the reservation across the border, he replied with a speech full of scorn and native dignity. It is still preserved.

"Look straight at me," he said, stretching his arms out to the north, the south, the east, and the west. "Do you know the cause of this war? You ask me if I am going to return. It is impossible for me to go back. God never told the Americans to come to the head of the Missouri. We were raised on this side of the sea. You were raised on the other side. . . . God made me big

enough, I know, because His Great Mother
covers me. My heart was made strong, but now
really it is weak, and that is why the Americans
want to lick my blood. Why do the Americans
want to drive me? Because they want only
Americans to be there. God made me leader of
the people, and that is why I am following the
buffalo. . . . If you will use your influence with
the President to send back the bad men to where
they came from, and leave the good men, there
will be peace."

This continued to be Sitting Bull's attitude
for the next four years. To an American com-
mission sent by General Terry, offering peace
terms, he replied curtly that "he did not trust the
'Long Knives.' They said one thing, and they
did another." It was not until the end of the
year 1880, and after he had learned that he and
his followers could not become British subjects,
that he laid down his arms and recrossed the
border.

Although he had surrendered in name to the
hated Americans, he was still irreconcilable. He
still dreamed of the day when he could muster
another army and drive them out. They were
interlopers, living on the land of his fathers.
He was confined as a prisoner of war in Fort
Randall until 1883, and then released but kept
under surveillance, at Standing Rock. Out-

wardly quiet, he reminded one of a tiger behind
bars.

The next seven years passed peacefully
enough, and then, in the fall of 1890, a curious
upheaval appeared. It was the "Messiah" craze
which captured the imaginations of hundreds of
Indians, and for a time threatened another war.
The head of this movement was Kicking Bear,
a fanatic from the Cheyenne Reservation, who
went about preaching a new religion which
should bring the Indians back into their inheri-
tance—something as the prophets of old in Israel
told of a great leader who was to come. It was
a doctrine as fascinating to the subjugated tribes
of Indians, as it had been to the lost tribes of
Israel.

One of the features of the new religion was
the "Ghost Dance," in which the whirling, writhing devotees would work themselves up into a
frenzy. Then Kicking Bear would harangue
them. A part of one of his speeches was reported
back to the military authorities, although the spy
who brought it repeated it with fear and trem-
bling. A dread as of the Black Hand was upon
him, should he be revealed as the informer. This
is a part of Kicking Bear's talk, as he reported
it:

"My brothers, I bring you the promise of a
day in which there will be no white man to lay his

hand on the bridle of the Indian's horse; when the red men of the prairie will rule the world and not be turned from the hunting grounds by any man. I bring you word from your fathers, the ghosts, that they are now marching to join you, led by the Messiah who came once to live on earth with the white men, but was cast out and killed by them. I have seen the wonders of the spirit-land, and have talked with the ghosts. I travelled far and am sent back with a message to tell you to make ready for the coming of the Messiah and return of the ghosts in the spring."

It is not strange to learn that Sitting Bull, grizzled old leader of the Sioux, was mixed up in this craze. Kicking Bear went to see him, and the old chief would have taken part in the ghost dances in person, had he not been prevented by the watchful soldiers. Not being allowed to attend, he sent some of his young men, who reported back to him every move of the new religion. Being more medicine man than warrior himself, it was exactly to his taste. He told Kicking Bear that he himself would act as high priest of the movement, and that he would organize ghost dances in the Standing Rock Reservation—which he forthwith did.

All over the Northwest there was unrest, and, according to Inspector McLaughlin, a bloody uprising was narrowly averted. "The spread of

news in the Indian country," he says, "is one of
those things not understandable of the white man.
And the coming of the Messiah was spread
among the Indians with the speed of the telegraph. It appeared one day among the Sho-
shones and Arapahoes in Wyoming, with a
personal Messiah up in the mountains in some
inaccessible place; the next day it was talked
of in Oklahoma, Nebraska, North and South
Dakota,—the Indians of widely distant localities
coming simultaneously to the knowledge of the
impending emancipation of the red men."

The ghost dances at Standing Rock were soon
attended by hundreds of shrieking Indians, both
male and female, who would dance until exhausted. One woman fell over unconscious at
the feet of the old chief, who sat silently watching
his followers. Bending over her, he pretended to
be listening to a message from the spirit-land,
from her lips. He was a born actor, and as he
repeated her fancied words, the dancers fairly
screamed with excitement. It was a hair-trigger
time, and the authorities realized that drastic
measures must be taken. Accordingly, General
Miles issued orders for the arrest of Sitting Bull,
and despatched Colonel William F. Cody—who
is much better known to fame as Buffalo Bill—
to make the arrest. At the reservation, however,
it was deemed best to entrust this duty to native

Indian police, so Buffalo Bill departed without taking part in it.

A company of blue-clad police, Crows and other friendly Indians, had been drilled at the Standing Rock Agency, and mightily proud they were of their uniform and prestige. To them was assigned the arrest of the old trouble-maker, and they rode out—thirty-nine in number—to his village, one crisp December morning.

Sitting Bull's band lived in houses scattered for some four or five miles along the bank of the Grand River. The two central houses were occupied by the old chief and his two wives. Riding directly up to these houses, a band of Indian police headed by Bull Head and Shave Head dismounted and entered. The old medicine man looked up as they opened the door, but did not move.

"You are under arrest," they said.

"Very well," he answered quietly enough, "I will go with you."

And heedless of his women, who began to cry and wring their hands, he rose and asked for his best blanket. He also asked that his best horse, a gray one, be saddled. Even as a prisoner, he wanted to look his best.

So quiet had it been in the house, that the soldiers were surprised, at the scene outside, when they emerged. From every direction the ghost-dancers and other followers came flying, to rescue their leader. Soon two or three hundred excited men and women were milling around the little band of soldiers, who stood unyielding, waiting for Sitting Bull to mount his horse and go with them. The old chief, however, was seemingly the most unconcerned of the lot. Throwing his blanket around his shoulders, he stalked toward his gray pony and placed his hand upon the pommel of the saddle. It is probable that he would have gone quietly, if at this tense moment an angry voice had not broken out high above the mutterings, like the hum of disturbed bees. It was the loud voice of Crow Foot, his son, shrill and full of reproach:

"You call yourself a brave man, and you have declared that you would never surrender to a blue-coat, and now you give yourself up to Indians in blue uniforms!" he shouted.

At the cutting taunt from his own son, Sitting Bull winced. To be publicly classed as a coward and by one's own household was more than Indian nature could endure. He glanced about, the old fire in his eye. He was hedged around by armed men, and his first hostile move meant death. But the outside circle was made up of his own followers, outnumbering the police four to one. Who knew? Perhaps this was indeed the opening scene of another war which, with himself as leader, might sweep from the Great River to the sea. His medicine had been good hitherto, and it ought not to desert him now, when the Indian need was so great. Flinging his blanket from him, he spread his arms wide and screamed:

"Shoot them! Kill them!"

At the command, shots rang out on all sides. He was enmeshed in a mob of writhing, cursing men,—then came darkness. A shot from one of his guards, striking him in the head, killed him instantly.

In the brief but bloody mêlée, discipline told, and the thirty-nine blue-coats dispersed the assailants, with six or eight killed on each side—one of them being Shave Head, leader of the police. To him and to his men were accorded military honors; and on that same winter day a military escort stood by as the body of Sitting Bull was also consigned to the bosom of his "Great Mother." His medicine had failed him at last, but I wonder if his unquiet ghost looking on and visioning the alternative—weary months and years in some military prison—might not have pronounced it "Good!"

CHAPTER FOURTEEN

DOWN in the southwestern part of the
United States,—long before the land
was so named,—and in northern Mexico, roamed for many years a nomadic tribe of
warriors whom their neighbors called "Apaches,"
or "Enemies," for it seemed as though, like Cain,
their hand was against every man's, and every
man's hand against them. The land itself was
for the most part desert, which was one reason
why the roving tribes so fiercely contested for
the choice spots. The Apaches really belonged
to the Navaho clan, and called themselves
"Inde," or "The People," in token of their superiority over others; but as far back as the year
1600, others called them Apaches, until they
came to adopt the name themselves.

And as far back as they can be traced, there
is a record of bloodshed; although they claim that
the Spanish conquistadors were the first aggres-
sors. The Indian legends are to the effect that
the natives welcomed the first explorers, and only
turned against them when the Spanish sought to

enslave them. Certain it is, that from the time
of the first Spanish colonization, the Apaches
were noted for their warlike disposition, raiding
white and Indian settlements alike. Geronimo,
the last of the fighting chiefs, died in captivity
at Fort Sill, Oklahoma, on February 17, 1909.
His story as told by himself is an epic of savag-
ery tempered by a burning sense of injustice, and
of its exact merits who can tell? This story was
told through an interpreter to Mr. S. M. Barrett,[1] and was viewed with such disapproval by
the War Department, that special permission
was obtained from President Theodore Roose-
velt to publish it.

It was in the year 1829, says Geronimo, that
he first saw the light of day, in Arizona, near
the headwaters of the Gila River. His father
was Taklishim, "The Gray One," and he was not
a chief, although his father—Geronimo's grandfather—had held that office. The boy's tribal
name was Goyathley, "One Who Yawns," and
he was not known as Geronimo ("Little
Jerome") until the Mexicans began to call him
that in derision. Soon, however, the name turned
from jest to deadly earnest, as the young warrior
began to show his mettle.

As a boy he roamed among the mountains
where the Gila had its source. In their fastnesses

[1] *Geronimo, the Story of His Life.*

the wigwams were hidden. Down in the valleys
were fertile lands for crops and for the grazing
of ponies. In the rocky caverns were the tribal
burying places. It was "home" for the lad and
his people, and his earliest recollections were of
rolling upon the dirt floor of his father's tepee,
or snugly fastened in the tsoch (cradle) upon
his mother's back, or hung therein to some gently
swaying limb of a tree. As he learned to talk,
his mother told him many stories of the sun, and
moon, and stars, and wild beasts. She also told
him of Usen, the one Great Spirit, who made
everything, and whom one should worship.

With his brothers and sisters the boy ran wild
for the first few years; but as soon as they were
old enough to be of service, all the children of
both sexes were put to work in the fields, cultivating the corn with wooden hoes, or pulling the
weeds. Many things grew in the warm, watered
valleys—melons, beans, corn, fruit, and tobacco,
but the chief crop was corn. Tobacco grew wild,
and the Apaches did not smoke it in pipes, as
did other Indians, but rolled it into cigarettes.
The corn was ground by hand, laboriously with
stone mortars and pestles, and thus made into
flour and cakes of bread. But sometimes the
kernels were soaked and allowed to ferment, and
a strong drink called "tis-win" made from it.
The children also gathered quantities of wild

berries and nuts, to add to the winter's store.
No one was idle, not even the men, who went over
the hills in search of game. Sometimes, however,
the children would get tired of the daily tasks
and decide quietly to go on a strike. They would
secretly plot to go away on a given day to some
spot several miles distant, and there spend the
entire day in a picnic. They were never punished for these escapades, but if by chance their
rendezvous was discovered, they were held up to
ridicule in the village.

When the tribe wanted to celebrate any event
such as a victory, a feast and dance would be
given. At times, some friendly neighboring tribe
would be invited. The festivities lasted for four
days. In the daytime they would eat to reple-
tion, and at night dance until they fell in their
tracks. At the end of the feasting there would
be horse-races, games, and athletic contests.
When Geronimo, as an old man, told of these
things, his face would light up, and he dwelt
again in memory upon those days which had gone
forever.

Their tribe was also religious, he averred. They
prayed to Usen, the One God, and were especially fervent if pestilence threatened their village.
But their brotherly love did not extend beyond
the borders of their own tribe; they thought it
no sin to kill any outsider. However, if by chance

one of their tribe accepted a favor from a stranger, that man became in a sense adopted into their
tribe and was protected. If any of the tribe
sinned against the others, the guilty ones were
not punished except to be banished from the
tribe. They became outlaws, and they it was—
so old Geronimo maintained—who committed
many of the depredations which were blamed
against the entire nation.

When the boy was only eight or nine years
old, he began to go hunting. There were great
herds of buffalo, antelope, elk, and deer, but the
Indians killed only what they needed. The buffalo were usually hunted on horseback, and slain
by arrows or spears. This was a man's job, and
Geronimo first learned to stalk the deer, by
crawling long distances from bush to bush, taking hours to creep close enough to launch his
arrow. Or perhaps it was wild turkeys or rabbits that the boys hunted. But strange to say,
they never went fishing. Though the waters
teemed with fish, the Apaches did not esteem
them as food. As Geronimo said, sententiously:
"Usen did not intend snakes, frogs, or fishes to
be eaten. I have never eaten of them."

As he grew older, he went out after bigger
game—the bears and the mountain lions—and
although his weapons were still only spears

and arrows, he was never injured in a fight with one of them.

Until he reached manhood, Geronimo had never seen a white man—even a missionary or a priest. His tribe, the Bedonkohe Apaches, lived rather quietly and peaceably, in their mountain retreat. But with manhood came a different story.

At the early age of seventeen he was admitted into the council of the warriors, which made him very happy, as now he could come and go at will, and sit in at the talks. He could also think about getting married, as many of the young braves married early. For a long time he had loved a girl of his tribe, called Alope. She was slender and delicate, but was the light of his eyes, nevertheless. He lost no time in asking her father for her hand. The old warrior put him off by saying that she was worth many ponies. Geronimo made no immediate reply to this, but in a few days was seen riding up again in a cloud of dust, driving a herd of ponies with him. He did not say where he got them, but ponies ran wild, and he may not have had to poach on another man's preserves. But in any event, the girl was his, and he rode proudly away with her. Although she was never strong she made him a good wife, and in due course three children were born to them.

Geronimo was nearly thirty before he went upon the warpath—according to his own story—and it was to avenge a private wrong. He and his tribe went down across the Mexican border to trade. They were then at peace with the dwellers in the small towns along the border, so they made camp a short distance away from a town and left only a small guard over their possessions and women and children. Most of the men rode into town to barter with the citizens. On their way back, they were met by some fugitive women from their camp, who told them that Mexican soldiers from another place had raided their party, captured all their ponies, seized their goods, and killed many of the women and children. On receipt of this shocking tidings, the braves quickly separated and stole up to their camp from different directions. When they got there, they found the report only too true. Among the slain were Geronimo's mother and his wife, Alope, and their three children. For a few minutes the young brave was stunned with grief. "There were no lights in camp," he said, "so without being noticed I silently turned away and stood by the river. How long I stood there I do not know, but when I saw the warriors arranging for a council I took my place."

This tragic moment marked the turning point in Geronimo's life. He never forgot the wrong done that day, and as long as he lived he hated the Mexicans with a fervent hatred. On the homeward march he was morose and silent. "There was nothing to say," he states. Home again, the broken band began to lay plans for revenge. Geronimo burned his lodge, with all his wife's things and his children's trinkets. He also burned the lodge of his mother, with all her belongings. Henceforth, he was a man of the open spaces, a firebrand of destruction. He volunteered and was appointed by his tribe as an emissary to other tribes to seek their aid in a campaign against the Mexicans. And so eloquently did he speak of his wrongs and those of his tribe, that within a few months three tribes had joined them on the warpath.

This time they traveled silently but swiftly. They were not mounted, as horses leave too plain a trail, and men on foot could dodge and twist about in the mountains so that none could follow them. They reached the town of Arispe, before the Mexicans were apprised of their approach. Then eight men were sent out to parley with them—only to be killed and scalped in plain sight of the astounded villagers. As the Indians intended, this was to draw out the whole force of the Mexicans for an open fight. It was successful, for two companies of cavalry and two of infantry were sent out the next morning against

them. Geronimo recognized in the cavalry some
of the very soldiers who had killed his family,
and the sight nerved his arm all the more. There
would be no quarter in this battle, he resolved.

And there was not. Never was a fight between
whites and Indians waged more fiercely. After
the first shock of surprise at seeing the Indians
standing firmly against their attack, the Mexicans settled grimly to the task of driving them
off the field, or cutting them down. Easier said
than done. The braves melted away as if by
magic at one point, only to appear in a formidable cluster elsewhere. They buzzed around the
soldiers like angry hornets.

Geronimo at this time was no chief, but he
knew the lay of the land and his desire for revenge was overmastering; so he was given charge
of the field of battle. He arranged his men in a
hollow circle near a river. They were sheltered
by timber. When the Mexicans advanced to dislodge them, he threw some of his men around to
attack them in the rear. The soldiers were thrown
into some confusion, but withstood the attack
bravely. The fighting lasted for two hours and
was fierce beyond description. They were like
wild animals springing at each other's throats.
At last in the center of the field were only eight
men—four braves and four soldiers. The arrows of the Indians were all gone, the spear-

heads broken off in the bodies of their enemies. Only their bare hands and small knives were left them. As they turned to face the soldiers, the latter fired and two Indians fell. Geronimo and the other brave turned and fled toward the rest of their tribe, at the edge of the timber. His companion was struck down, but Geronimo seized a spear from one of the others, and transfixed the nearest of the pursuing four. With the enemy's saber, which Geronimo quickly grasped, he faced the onslaught of the next soldier, and soon killed him also. Then dripping with blood, Geronimo turned to find the other soldiers; but they had fled. His companions had seen his feat of arms, however, and filled the air with their exultant whoops. The victory was theirs, and although many of their own number lay upon the field, they rejoiced that the former massacre was avenged. And then and there they chose Geronimo as the war chief of their tribes.

This was the way in which he rose to power, and soon his name began to be bruited abroad with respect and fear. For having tasted of blood, he was not content again to go back to the paths of peace. He planned a series of minor raids upon Mexican towns, sometimes going with twenty men, sometimes with even fewer. They would strike quickly, kill any in their path, steal horses, and then scatter into the mountains. For several years this continued, and the Mexicans in reprisal attacked an Apache village, in the winter of 1861, slaying the inhabitants, of both sexes and all ages. Geronimo was not in this fight, but in many another; during the course of the next few years he was wounded seven times, and once given up for dead.

The border at this time was the scene of much lawlessness. The Civil War was raging in the East, so few American soldiers were here in the far Southwest. Instead, there were many desperadoes, both Mexican and American. Cattle were stolen on all sides, and other raids and fights were common. Geronimo as an old man stoutly maintained that a great many of these outrages were committed by the white men, but that all were blamed upon the Apaches. Up to this time, the activities of the Indians had been chiefly directed against the Mexicans; the Indians making dashes across the border and returning with booty—if they were successful—to their haunts in Arizona.

At the close of the war in the East, companies of American soldiers were stationed in different posts in the West, some being in Arizona Territory, as it was then called. There were some clashes, as a matter of course, with the wandering Apache bands, and soon the Indians grew to hate the Americans quite as cordially as they had hated the Mexicans. The natives felt that they were gradually being driven from their own land, and that even when treaties were made they were not lived up to, by the Americans—charges which were only too true.

The culminating blow against the Indians came in an inhuman massacre, at Camp Grant, in the spring of 1871. During the winter preceding, small bands of Apaches had drifted in to the post for protection and food. They said that they wanted peace and a place to live undisturbed. The officer in charge, Lieutenant Whitman, took an interest in them, and gave them a place for their tepees and issued rations to them. In the weeks that followed, their numbers gradually increased to several hundred, and he became well acquainted with them. "They had so won on me," he wrote in his official report, which is still on file in the War Department, "that from my first idea of treating them justly and honestly, as an officer of the army, I had come to feel a strong personal interest in helping to show them the way to a higher civilization. I had come to feel respect for men who, ignorant and naked, were still ashamed to lie or steal."

On the morning of April 30, Whitman received word that a large party of white men— not soldiers—had left Tucson, with the avowed purpose of killing all the Indians at his post.

The Indians had been living in peace and under his eye for weeks, but the white desperadoes wanted to "clear the country of Indians," and this was one means of doing it. The lieutenant had only a small body of men, some fifty raw recruits, and before he could reach the Indian village, the massacre had been accomplished. "I could find no living Indians," he writes. "Their camp was burning, and the ground strewn with their dead and mutilated women and children."

The white ruffians had departed, and the officer set his men to work burying the bodies of the victims. "While we were at the work, many of them (the survivors) came to the spot and indulged in expressions of grief too wild and terrible to be described. That evening they began to come in from all directions, singly and in small parties, so changed as hardly to be recognizable in the forty-eight hours during which they had neither eaten nor slept. Many of the men, whose families had been killed, when I spoke to them and expressed sympathy for them, were obliged to turn away, unable to speak, and too proud to show their grief. The women whose children had been killed or stolen were convulsed with grief, and looked at me appealingly, as if I were their last hope on earth. Children, who two days before had been full of frolic, kept at a distance, expressing wondering horror.

"Their camp was surrounded and attacked at daybreak. So sudden and unexpected was it, that I found a number of women shot while asleep beside their bundles of hay, which they had collected to bring in that morning. One of the chiefs said: 'I no longer want to live; my women and children have been killed before my face, and I have been unable to defend them.' "

One hundred and twenty-five or more were killed in cold blood in this unwarranted massacre. An army surgeon, who was called in to attend the survivors, filed an official report at Washington deploring the attack. He said it was absolutely unjustified. "I have never seen any Indians who showed the intelligence, honesty, and desire to learn manifested by these Indians," he ended. "I came among them greatly prejudiced against them; but after being with them, I was compelled to admit that they were honest in their intentions, and really desired peace."

Geronimo makes no mention of this massacre, as he tells only of events in which he was personally concerned. But the news spread as quickly as though by telegraph among the tribes and did not lessen their uneasiness, if not positive hostility. When he sent his young men out after recruits, he could always find them; and thus it was that for ten or more years the border ran red with blood. Even when truces were patched

up with the warring Apaches, they were but tem-
porary; first one side, then the other broke the
treaties—and it was as apt to be the white man
as the Indian.

One of the wrongs suffered at the hands of the
white men, which made Geronimo especially vin-
dictive, was the killing of their tribal head-chief,
Mangus-Colorado. He with three other chiefs
went of their own accord to a settlement in New
Mexico, to make a treaty of peace, and Mangus
after being lured by promises into the white camp
was held as prisoner and slain during the night.
General Nelson A. Miles in an official report
confirmed this, saying: "Mangus-Colorado had
been foully murdered after he had surrendered."

Geronimo was then made head-chief, and lost
no time in wreaking vengeance on the first white
people he could get his hands upon. They proved
to be four cowboys with a herd of cattle. The
cowboys were set upon and killed, but not
scalped as "they were not warriors." Then the
Indians fled to Apache Pass. They were pursued by soldiers and, about ten days later, a running fight ensued, which lasted all day. When
the Indians' arrows and spears were all gone,
they dismounted and scattered on foot among the
rocks, where the soldiers could not follow.

This was only the first of many skirmishes,
while Geronimo stayed on the warpath. He

varied these adventures by occasional raids across
the border against his ancient enemies, the
Mexicans. At one time, his tribe made peace
and was given grazing lands on a reservation.
But again trouble broke out, the Indians claim-
ing that they had been deprived of their water
rights. It was not until the year 1882 that the
old warrior with a picked band of braves, fresh
from a foray in Sonora, Mexico, was surrounded
by General Crook's men and forced to surrender.
Geronimo was given one of the best farms in
San Carlos, and for a time it really looked as
though he had settled down to a peaceful old
age; but again trouble followed. He had made
some tis-win, the native drink brewed from corn,
and when the authorities heard of it and attempted to stop him, he flew into a rage and
again daubed himself with warpaint.

During 1884 and 1885 his name was once more
a terror along the border, and the word came
from Washington, "Get Geronimo, dead or
alive!" General Miles, who had been placed at
the head of the frontier forces, sent a party of
soldiers hot foot on the old "outlaw's" trail. They
pursued him down into Mexico—disregarding a
little thing like international boundary lines—
and finally made it so hot for him that he sent
word to Miles he was ready to surrender. The
general agreed to a parley, and the old chief rode

up to him, with a few of his braves, saluted and dismounted. The report of that colloquy in the Indian's own words is most interesting. He recited the wrongs which he and his people had suffered at the hands of the white men, and said that all they desired now was a homeland where they could live undisturbed with their families and herds. The general replied that the President, at Washington, had heard of their wrongs and would give them good land, well timbered and watered, and afford them protection from their enemies. But the Indians must promise on their part to change their thoughts to peace.

"Then I agreed," says Geronimo, "and gave up my arms. I said: 'I will quit the warpath and live at peace hereafter.'

"Then General Miles swept a spot of ground clear with his hand, and said: 'Your past deeds shall be wiped out like this, and you will start a new life.'"

Instead of being placed upon a reservation, as Geronimo was led to believe, he and some three hundred and forty other Apaches were shipped east to Florida, where they were kept as prisoners of war and put to hard labor, sawing logs. This lasted for about two years, and then they were transferred to a prison in Alabama. Meanwhile, the old chief appealed in vain to the authorities in Washington to respect the terms of the treaty made with Miles. The spot where they were now held was low and unhealthful, and some of the prisoners died. Two committed suicide. At last they were sent back across the Mississippi— to Fort Sill, Oklahoma. This was in 1894, and was the last move of these unfortunate people. Here they met with better treatment. Although still technically prisoners of war, they were given farms, houses, and livestock,—cattle, hogs, turkeys, and chickens.

"The Indians did not do much good with the hogs," said Geronimo himself, in telling his experiences to S. M. Barrett, who put his life-story into book form, "because they did not understand how to care for them, and not many Indians even at the present time keep hogs. We did better with the turkeys and chickens, but with these we did not have as good luck as white men do. With the cattle we have done very well, indeed, and we like to raise them. We have a few horses also, and we have had no bad luck with them."

The Apaches and other Indians proved, in fact, what they had maintained all along—that they were capable of managing their own affairs and living at peace with the rest of the world, if the rest of the world would live at peace with them. But how many long, weary years of bloodshed it required to prove this fact to both sides!

As for Geronimo, the last of the fighting Apaches, he passed away at a ripe old age, at peace with the world. He professed Christianity, in 1903, and dearly loved to deck himself out on Sunday in his best—which was the garb of the white man, and not buckskin and feathers—and go to the Dutch Reformed Church, on the reservation. He died in 1909, at the age of eighty, with but one final wish, that his people should return to the home of their fathers.

"If this cannot be done during my lifetime," he said, in closing the dramatic story of his life, "if I must die in bondage—I hope that the remnant of the Apache tribe may, when I am gone, be granted the one privilege which they request —to return to Arizona."

EAU CLAIRE STATE TEACHERS COLLEGE
LIBRARY RULES

No book should be taken from the library until it has been properly charged by the librarian.

Books may be kept two weeks but are not to be renewed without special permission of the librarian.

A fine of two cents a day will be charged for books kept over time.

In case of loss or injury the person borrowing this book will be held responsible for a part or the whole of the value of a new book.

DUE	DUE	DUE	DUE
Mar 20 '53	Jl 19 57	OCT 30 '72	
Jul 23 '54	Feb 18 '58	APR 25 '73	
Oct 20 '54	Feb 13 '59		
	Nov 6 '59		
Nov 11 '54	Jun 29 '61		
May 25 '55	Dec 17 '62		
Oct 24 '55	May 1 63		
Nov 15 '55	Nov 1		
	Nov 1		
Jun 22 '5	Nov 12 '68		
Jul 13	Jl 3 '70		
Oct 22	NOV 30 '70		
May 8 57	SE 8 '71		
8 57	NOV 3 1971		
	OCT 18 '72		